THE BEATLES
REVEALED

© 2010 The Foundry Creative Media Company Ltd

This edition published by World Publications Group, Inc.
by arrangement with The Foundry Creative Media Company Ltd.

World Publications Group, Inc.
140 Laurel Street
East Bridgewater, MA 02333
www.wrldpub.com

Publisher and Creative Director: Nick Wells
Project Editor and Picture Research: Sara Robson
Art Director: Mike Spender
Layout Design: Rob Fletcher and Jake
Digital Design and Production: Chris Herbert and Jake

Special thanks to: Helen Crust, Chelsea Edwards, Amanda Leigh, Geoffrey Meadon, Polly Prior and Digby Smith

All rights reserved. No part of this publication may be reproduced or transmitted, in any form or by any means, electronic, mechanical,
photocopying, recording or otherwise, without the prior permission in writing of the publisher.

Every effort has been made to contact copyright holders. We apologize in advance for any omissions and would be pleased to insert the
appropriate acknowledgement in subsequent editions of this publication.

Hugh Fielder (Author) can remember the 1960s even though he was there. He can remember the 1970s and 1980s because he was at *Sounds*
magazine (RIP) and the 1990s because he was editor of Tower Records' *TOP* magazine. He has shared a spliff with Bob Marley, a glass of wine
with David Gilmour, a pint with Robert Plant, a cup of tea with Keith Richards and a frosty stare with Axl Rose. He has watched Mike Oldfield strip
naked in front of him and Bobby Womack fall asleep while he was interviewing him.

PAUL DU NOYER (Introduction) began his career on the *New Musical Express*, went on to edit *Q* and to found *Mojo*. He also helped to launch
Heat and several music websites. As well as editing several rock reference books, he is the author of *We All Shine On*, about the solo music of
John Lennon, and *Wondrous Place*, a history of the Liverpool music scene. He is nowadays a contributing editor of *The Word*.

Picture Credits
Alamy Images: Avico Ltd: 144–45; David Ball: 182–83; Tom Hanley: 196–97; Interfoto: 16–17, 118; Trinity Mirror/Mirrorpix: 164; Werner Otto: 123; Pictorial Press Ltd: 43, 124, 176, 179, 193.
Corbis: Atlantide Phototravel: 13; Bettmann: 184–85; Douglas Kirkland: 178. **Foundry Arts:** 40, 51 (l), 62 (r), 81 (l), 83, 90 (t), 97 (r), 99 (l), 103, 114 (t), 115, 119 (t), 122 (tl), 139 (l), 150 (l),
177 (t). **Getty Images:** CBS Photo Archive: 68–69; Hulton Archive: 19, 42, 50, 51 (r), 57, 59, 60–61, 64, 65, 66, 76–77, 80, 91, 96–97, 98, 110–11, 113, 116–17, 120–21, 125, 126–27,
128–29, 147, 148, 152, 155, 168–69, 170, 172–73, 177 (b), 180, 194 (l); New York Daily News: 67, 99 (r), 100, 122 (b); Terry O'Neill: 48–49; Michael Ochs Archives: 20, 23, 30, 35, 36, 70
(b), 71, 81 (r), 109, 154, 158, 160, 190, 194 (r); Popperfoto: 22, 37, 41, 54, 90 (b), 95, 108, 142; Premium Archive: 102; Redferns: 12, 21, 24–25, 26 (t), 26 (b), 27, 28–29, 31, 32–33, 34,
38–39, 45, 74, 78–79, 83 (tl), 86–87, 89, 112, 122 (tr), 131, 133, 138, 140–41, 143 (tl), 143, 156–57, 166–67, 174, 175, 181, 187, 191, 195; Bob Thomas Sports Photography: 62 (l), 63,
72–73; Time & Life Pictures: 18, 70 (t), 159; Roger Viollet: 119 (b); WireImage: 114 (b). **London Features International:** 44, 146, 149, 153. **Mirrorpix:** 15, 52, 53, 55, 56, 58, 75, 82, 83 (b),
84, 85, 88, 92, 93, 94, 101, 104, 105, 126 (l), 130, 132, 134, 135, 136, 137, 139 (r), 150–51, 161, 165, 168 (l), 171, 186, 188, 189. **TopFoto:** 14, 192, 196 (l).

ISBN: 978-1-57215-880-1

Printed and bound in China

11 13 15 14 12
1 3 5 7 9 8 6 4 2

THE BEATLES REVEALED

BY HUGH FIELDER
INTRODUCTION BY PAUL DU NOYER

JG PRESS

Contents

Introduction

There are so many books stuffed with learned theories about The Beatles, that we can easily overlook the point that really matters. Simply, The Beatles were the greatest device that was ever invented for causing enjoyment on a global scale. There used to be a record label whose half-ironical slogan was 'Happy to be Part of the Industry of Human Happiness'. But that is exactly what The Beatles were. A sort of Happiness Machine. In a career that now looks astonishingly brief – all their LPs were made between 1963 and 1970 – they gave the world an abundance of delight. And as new generations discover, The Beatles' music is a gift that goes on giving. There is no law that orders us to love the songs of John, Paul, George and Ringo – but it's practically impossible not to.

On the group's 1964 album, *Beatles For Sale*, there is an irresistible sleevenote by their droll, far-sighted press agent Derek Taylor. 'When, in a generation or so,' he writes, 'a radio-active, cigar-smoking child, picnicking on Saturn, asks you what the Beatle affair was all about – Did you actually *know* them? – don't try to explain all about the long hair and the screams! Just play the child a few tracks from this album and he'll probably understand what it was all about. The kids of AD 2000 will draw from the music much the same sense of well being and warmth as we do today.'

All right, so the colourful sci-fi scene is a little off course, but as AD 2000 itself recedes into history, the general truth of Taylor's prediction is unassailable. For people who grew up in the 1960s, when The Beatles were in the very fabric of everyday life, those songs are intensely nostalgic. But much of the group's colossal fanbase today was not even born when the last dying chords of 'Let It Be' were recorded. Nostalgia alone cannot explain the seeming immortality of The Beatles' appeal. Their art belongs to the ages, not just to the aged.

Great as it was, perhaps the music is not the only reason for that enduring fascination. There is something about The Beatles' *story* – a fairy-tale quality in their rise, a certain tragic drama in

their fall – that captures our imaginations. In the seven years between their first hits and the eventual split, The Beatles changed the course of popular music, probably for ever. They were figureheads for the most profound social changes of that century. And in their own lives, those four young men experienced extremes of fame, adulation, hostility, self-doubt and recrimination.

As a narrative alone, The Beatles' story is amazing. Throw in the soundtrack – that unsurpassable, life-enhancing soundtrack – and we have the most compelling package in the history of entertainment. No wonder we can't seem to get enough of The Beatles.

The innovations began with the group's first singles, all self-written in a time when that was rare. Follow-up albums confirmed the presence of an awesome team in John Lennon and Paul McCartney. *With The Beatles*, in particular, took the spirit of American R&B and fused it with something fresh, young and distinctively British. The screaming soon began, 'Beatlemania' was coined and the bedlam was exported across the globe. Pop music has rarely sounded so joyful and confident as in The Beatles' celebratory anthems 'She Loves You' and 'I Want To Hold Your Hand'. The boys' long hair was an extraordinary sight, however tame it looks to later generations, and the shockwaves of the band's success were felt far outside the hit parade. Above all were their attitudes: down-to-earth, classless and cheeky. Fans saw them as deities. All they tried to be was ordinary.

At first the four Beatles seemed identikit, a single mop-topped entity, but after their movie debut *A Hard Day's Night*, individual personalities emerged: sharp-tongued John, heart-throb Paul,

laid-back George, lovably daft Ringo. These were caricatures that the group never quite shook off, but they did no harm. Aristocrats and statesmen sought their company, while intellectuals praised their artistry and pondered their significance. At a time of upheaval, The Beatles were swiftly identified with the Western youth movement, though no age group was immune to their charm. All the while, behind the Iron Curtain, their works were circulated like talismans of forbidden freedom. Despite so many distractions, the records were never formulaic and grew in complexity at dizzying speed. *Rubber Soul*, in 1965, was perhaps the first rock album that people seriously considered as art.

But as pioneers The Beatles were also the first to discover pitfalls. Such staggering success could not escape the backlash of controversy, especially when they spoke their minds on war, religion, drugs and anything they were asked about. Their world became a dangerous place to travel in, and one night in 1966, they played their last ever public show. In fact the decision was not a retreat, but an advance, because they could now make the recording studio their natural habitat and raise our idea of rock's possibilities even higher. *Revolver* and *Sgt. Pepper's Lonely Hearts Club Band* were arguably The Beatles at their creative zenith.

The velocity of change was incredible. To contrast The Beatles of, say, 1963, with the band of 1968, is to sense the cultural vertigo they always provoked. Whether in lyrics and sound, in fashion or philosophy, nothing was fixed. No wonder The Beatles fed a belief that rock music was hurtling forwards with irreversible momentum into an unimaginable future. Yet it was The Beatles, too, who first indicated some flaws in the plan....

The film of *A Magical Mystery Tour*, the band's own creation, revealed their limitations as conceptualists. Though the songs were undeniably brilliant, the movie was a dud. The passing, in 1967, of their manager Brian Epstein may have mattered more than anyone realized. Their next LP *The Beatles*, known as 'the White Album', was sprawling and disjointed. Naturally there were many flashes of genius, but its uneven texture betrayed a tailing off in the band's collective attention span, as well as a growing tendency for John, Paul and George to operate in artistic isolation from each other. The next movie project, *Yellow Submarine*, failed to engage the group at all.

As Harrison grew restless and resentful of his junior status, and Lennon was more energized by the avant-garde ideas of his new partner Yoko Ono, it fell to McCartney to explore some way of reviving The Beatles' focus. It was telling, however, that their only common ground was a return to the rock'n'roll values of Hamburg and the Cavern. The storming but explicitly retro single 'Get Back', and the laboured efforts to rehearse a stripped-down live act – recorded and filmed as *Let It Be* – were symptoms of a band who had given up looking forward. Whatever they saw, through the gun smoke of their post-Epstein business battles, was too upsetting to contemplate.

By 1969 The Beatles' career had completed its cycle. You can trace it in the music they had made since 1962, from youthful vigour and simplicity, through cleverness and formal perfection, to maturity and fatigue. *Let It Be* was their attempt to re-enter that early state of innocence, but it failed. 'Get Back' was a call for renewal, but the cycle could not turn a second time. Happily, the group's very last collaboration was *Abbey Road* (even if, confusingly, it was released before *Let It Be*), which was a stirring finale to the most glorious catalogue in pop music and a true collective effort that showed all four members to best effect.

Their solo careers began immediately. John Lennon's, in fact, was already under way. And if the results have nearly always been inferior to The Beatles, they are still quite frequently superb. But The Beatles, in any case, have never really disappeared. Successive re-issues and compilations (nowadays in formats undreamt of back in the 1960s), books and documentaries, even computer games, keep their name before our gaze. The Beatle 'brand' (another term they would not have recognized) has never left the upper reaches of the entertainment earnings table.

Being The Beatles took a lot out of them as individuals, even as it made them wealthy and famous. By their final photos, the four Fabs (not yet in their thirties) looked like Old Testament prophets. They had seen more than most human beings ever see, and the weariness of a hundred lifetimes was in their gaze. Their long hair and beards were no longer the symbols of youth and freedom but of hard experience and the burdens of tribal kingship. It's not too much to suggest we owe them a great debt of gratitude. We may or we may not see their like again. The Beatles embodied too much optimism, and generosity of spirit, for anyone to say that no one else will ever surpass their brilliance. In the meantime, we have the music and that will never let us down.

1957-62

Liverpool's most famous sons, the Beatles, were wartime babies: Richard Starkey (Ringo Starr) born 7 July 1940; John Winston Lennon born 9 October 1940; James Paul McCartney born 18 June 1942; and George Harrison born 24 February 1943. All four families moved at least once at the end of the war as Liverpool was rebuilt and renovated. They were not immune from other social upheavals in the post-war years, either. Lennon never knew his sailor father and grew up with his aunt Mimi. His mother Julia lived nearby with a new husband. Ringo's parents had separated when he was three.

All four Beatles were also part of Britain's first generation of 'teenagers', a term that had not existed before the war. By 1955 they had become a recognizable social group, looking to find their own entertainment. What brought the Beatles together was skiffle, a musical craze that was easy to imitate on cheap instruments. John Lennon formed a band, The Quarry Men, in 1957. A year later Paul McCartney and George Harrison were in the group. Sometimes the gigs dried up but they persevered. The line-up stabilized into the Beatles with the arrival of Lennon's friend Stuart Sutcliffe on bass, but they only got permanent drummer, Pete Best, just before they took up an offer to play a residency in a Hamburg Club in 1960. It was a tough experience but they survived (apart from Sutcliffe) and back in Liverpool they soon became the leading band on the scene.

The real turning point came when Brian Epstein became the Beatles' manager. He smartened them up, got them a record-company audition and finally a contract. He also, at the band's behest, fired drummer Pete Best and installed Ringo. Now it was up to them....

Pre 1957

Beatles' Schooldays

John Lennon and George Harrison attended the same primary school although, three years apart, they never met. The first two Beatles to meet were Harrison and Paul McCartney who had passed the 11-plus exam and gone to the Liverpool Institute. They regularly caught the same bus back to Speke and would often hang out at Harrison's house strumming their guitars. Lennon had failed his 11-plus and gone to Quarry Bank High School where he continued to fail academically. Ringo, meanwhile, had spent almost as much time in hospital as school with peritonitis, pleurisy and various lung ailments.

1957

Spring: Origins Of The Quarry Men

The skiffle craze that swept Britain in the mid-Fifties, spearheaded by Lonnie Donegan, was a defining influence on all four Beatles. They badgered their parents for cheap acoustic guitars and strummed clumsily along to songs like 'Cumberland Gap' and 'Rock Island Line'. John Lennon, a rebel looking for a cause, was the first to form a band, The Quarry Men, in the spring of 1957. It was a six-piece band that included a banjo and a tea-chest bass, although the personnel changed frequently as members found John's volatile temperament hard to handle.

May: Early Shows

After an informal performance at a British Empire Day street party in Rose Street, Woolton, on 22 May 1957, The Quarry Men, perhaps over-ambitiously, auditioned for the local TV talent show *Star Search* at the Liverpool Empire on 9 June. Not surprisingly they failed that audition, and another for a lunchtime spot at the Cavern Club, at that time a jazz club in a dank cellar beneath a warehouse in Mathew Street. Their first 'proper' gig was at another street party in Rosebery Street on 22 June. They played on the back of a lorry while the microphone lead was fed through the window of No. 76.

July: When John Met Paul

Paul McCartney showed up at the next Quarry Men gig, a garden fête at St Peter's Church, Woolton, on 6 July, invited by a friend who also knew John Lennon and introduced them. 'As he leaned an arm on my shoulder I realized he was drunk,' McCartney remembered. 'John was obviously leading this thing. He didn't know the words or anything. He'd obviously heard the records and not bought them.' Lennon remembered playing 'Be-Bop-A-Lula' for the first time. After the show McCartney auditioned, playing 'Twenty Flight Rock' on Lennon's guitar (upside down because he was left-handed) and impressed Lennon by knowing the words. McCartney passed the audition but he was still on holiday when The Quarry Men played their one and only Cavern Club show. Mid-way through the owner passed a note onstage: 'Cut out the bloody rock'. McCartney's first gig was at the New Clubmoor Hall, Norris Green, on 18 October. 'A disaster. I got sticky fingers.'

1958

February: George Joins

Despite his friendship with Paul McCartney, George Harrison didn't get to see The Quarry Men until 6 February at the Wilson Hall, Garston. 'I remember being very impressed with John's big thick sideboards and Teddy Boy clothes.' He did an impromptu audition on the bus home. A few days later McCartney asked Lennon what he thought. 'He gave it a second or two and then he replied, "Yeah man, he'd be great". And that was it, George was in.' From the outset George played lead while John and Paul played rhythm guitars.

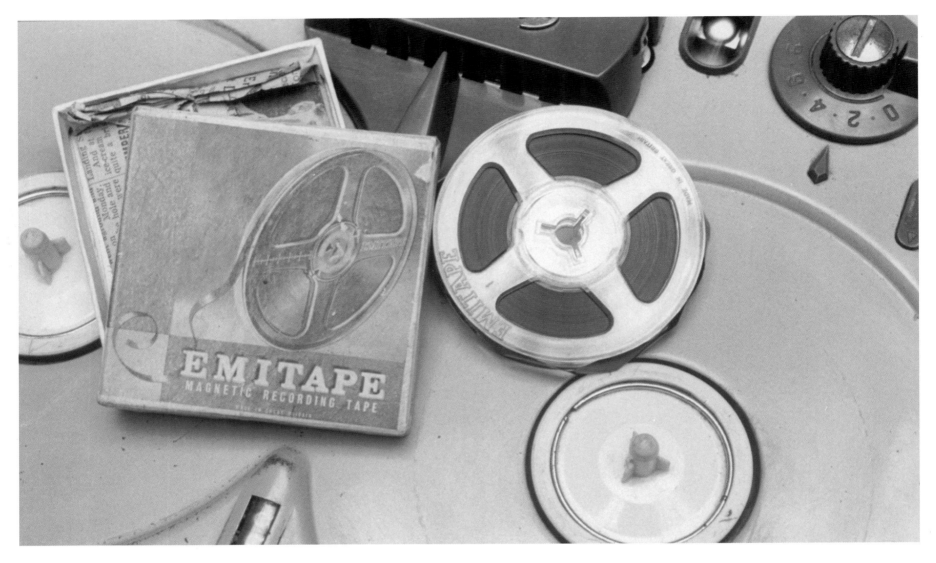

June & July: First Recording

In the summer of 1958 The Quarry Men: John Lennon, Paul McCartney and George Harrison plus John 'Duff' Lowe on piano and Colin Hanton on drums, recorded two songs at the grandly named Phillips' Sound Recording Services, actually Peter Phillips' living room at 38 Kensington, Liverpool. They cut Buddy Holly's 'That'll Be The Day' and a McCartney/Harrison song, 'In Spite Of All The Danger', onto a 78 rpm acetate that each Quarry Man kept for a week. John Lowe kept it for 23 years, before deciding to auction it; Paul McCartney stepped in and bought it. He had engineers restore the sound as much as possible and pressed 50 copies for family and friends. The songs were publicly released on The Beatles' 1995 *Anthology 1*.

1959

January: Beginning Of Lennon And McCartney

The gigs started drying up for The Quarry Men in the autumn of 1958 and by January 1959 there was nothing on the horizon. John Lennon had also been devastated by the death of his mother, killed by a speeding car. George Harrison drifted off to join the Les Stewart Quartet but Lennon, who was now attending Liverpool Art College, and McCartney hung together, practising and writing songs. Early efforts included 'Love Me Do' which would become their first single, 'Hello Little Girl' and 'Love Of The Loved' which would be hits for The Fourmost and Cilla Black, and 'One After 909' that would eventually come out on The Beatles' final album, *Let It Be* (1970).

August: Johnny & The Moondogs

The Quarry Men returned briefly in August when the Les Stewart Quartet broke up acrimoniously just hours before they were due to play the opening night of the Casbah Club in West Derby. George Harrison and fellow guitarist Ken Brown hurriedly recruited Lennon and McCartney and they played as The Quarry Men. They played well enough to be offered a weekly residency until they walked out a few months later after a row about money. They also had another shot at Carroll Levis' *Star Search*, disguising their previous appearance by calling themselves Johnny & The Moondogs. This time they progressed to the final heat, held at Manchester's Hippodrome Theatre, but they flunked out when they had to catch the last train back to Liverpool, missing their final slot that included the all-important 'Clapometer'.

1960

May: Stuart Sutcliffe Joins

Although the bookings had dried up again at the beginning of 1960, John's art school friend Stuart Sutcliffe was persuaded to join the band on bass. Having sold a painting for £65 he was able to buy a big, stylish Hofner bass that he couldn't actually play. But no matter; it looked good and he could learn to play as the four of them continued to rehearse and practise new songs. Stuart also brought a new name for the group: The Beetles. But what good was a name without gigs?

May: Johnny Gentle Tour

The Beetles' prospects improved in May when Allan Williams, owner of the Jacaranda coffee bar, a hang-out for local bands, became their part-time manager. He rechristened them The Silver Beetles, found them a drummer, Tommy Moore, gave them a regular spot at his club and secured them an audition with impresario Larry Parnes to back his protégé, Liverpudlian Billy Fury (pictured on the far left). Parnes had reservations but a few days later offered the group a job backing Johnny Gentle (pictured on the left), another young Liverpudlian, on a tour of the Scottish Highlands. The tour was not a success but the experience was invaluable.

Summer: Liverpool Gigs

Back in Liverpool, The Silver Beetles found themselves booked on a series of dancehall gigs across the Mersey. They played at the notoriously rough Neston Institute and the even rougher Grosvenor Ballroom in Wallasey where Stuart Sutcliffe was badly beaten up one night, an event that probably caused his brain haemorrhage a couple of years later. But they couldn't hang on to drummer Tommy Moore who opted for the life (and wage) of a fork-lift truck driver rather than enduring John Lennon's caustic comments.

July: Janice The Stripper

Drummer-less once more, The Silver Beetles were in no position to refuse Allan Williams' unlikely offer: backing a stripper called Janice at an illegal strip club he'd opened. Paul McCartney recalled, 'We played behind Janice and at the end of her act she would turn round and … well, we were all young lads, we'd never seen anything like it before, and all blushed … Four blushing red-faced lads.' McCartney covered some of his blushes by playing drums.

August: Pete Best Joins

Finally The Silver Beetles got a break. In early August Allan Williams was asked to supply a band to play at the Indra Club in Hamburg, Germany. He offered it to the band if they could find a drummer. A few days later the band were in the Casbah Club on a night off where they found the owner's son, Pete Best, playing with The Blackjacks. Even better, The Blackjacks were splitting up. They asked Best if he wanted to go to Hamburg. Then they asked if he wanted to join the band. Somehow Best passed the hurriedly-arranged audition for the band that was now renamed The Beatles.

August: First Hamburg Trip

On 16 August Allan Williams drove The Beatles to Hamburg where they signed a contract for a 48-night residency at the Indra Club, just off the Reeperbahn in the city's red light district. They played five hours a night, six on Saturdays and Sundays, and slept in two squalid rooms behind the screen of a nearby cinema. After complaints about the noise, the club was closed and they moved to the larger Kaiserkeller where the owner exhorted them to 'Make show, make show' to entertain the punters. They duly livened up their act, fuelled by a diet of amphetamines and beer. As George Harrison said, 'Our sound really stems from Germany. That's where we learned to work for hours and hours on end and keep on working at full peak even though we reckoned our legs and arms were about ready to drop off.'

December: The Beatles Return Home

When The Beatles unilaterally transferred their affections from the Kaiserkeller to the rival Top Ten Club, the Kaiserkeller owner duly took revenge. First he had George Harrison deported for being underage, and then had Paul McCartney and Pete Best deported for arson. In December the band made their separate ways back to Liverpool, apart from Stuart Sutcliffe who remained with his new girlfriend, photographer Astrid Kirchherr, who took the first iconic pictures of The Beatles. Sutcliffe had never really learned to play his bass which had become a point of friction in the band.

December: Bringing Hamburg To Liverpool

Back in Liverpool, the four remaining Beatles regrouped and, with stand-in bass player Chas Newby, played a gig at Litherland Town Hall on 27 December. Their Hamburg-style show was an instant success and the promoter promptly rebooked them for a string of shows. But when Newby stood down they were forced to confront the bassist issue from within their own ranks; Paul McCartney drew what was considered the short straw. The Beatles were now a quartet. In the first three months of 1961 they played more than 80 shows, including residencies at the Casbah Club and the Cavern, which had wisely changed its music policy. They became the hottest band in Liverpool and the first screams at a Beatle gig were heard. John Lennon recalled 'We discovered we were quite famous. This was when we began to think we were good.'

1961

March: Second Hamburg Stint

The Beatles returned to Hamburg at the end of March for a three-month residency at the Top Ten Club. The money was marginally better and Paul McCartney was able to afford to buy his first trademark Hofner violin-shaped bass, but the hours were longer: seven hours a night, eight at weekends. Sometimes they shared the bill with another Liverpool band, Rory Storm & The Hurricanes and found themselves getting chummy with their drummer, Ringo Starr. They also remained friends with Stuart Sutcliffe and were so impressed by his black leather suit that they had their own made.

June: Sheridan Sessions

The first 'official' recording session by The Beatles took place during their second Hamburg stint when they backed Tony Sheridan, another English singer plying his trade in Germany. Over two days they recorded a dozen or so songs produced by Bert Kaempfert (who would go on to become a major star himself) for Polydor Records. A rocked-up version of the traditional Scottish folk song 'My Bonnie Lies Over The Ocean', retitled 'My Bonnie', was released as a single and reached No. 5 in the German charts at the end of 1961. It was credited to Tony Sheridan & The Beat Brothers as the word 'Beatles' was a little too close to 'Pidels', German slang for penis. During the sessions The Beatles were allowed to cut two songs on their own: a lively version of 'Ain't She Sweet' sung by John Lennon and an instrumental by Lennon and Harrison called 'Cry For A Shadow'. Both tracks were promptly buried in Polydor's vaults but rapidly exhumed and shamelessly exploited when Beatlemania burst a couple of years later.

October: Birth Of The Mop Top

It was Astrid Kirchherr, Stuart Sutcliffe's girlfriend, who first encouraged The Beatles to comb their hair forward to give them a more identifiable image. John Lennon and Paul McCartney made a half-hearted attempt with the hairstyle but when the pair of them went on holiday to Paris in October and met another photographer friend from Hamburg, Jürgen Vollmer, they saw how it could really work. They soon persuaded George Harrison to follow suit but Pete Best resolutely refused to change the quiff that was his selling point with the girls.

December: Play Aldershot Palais

For the second half of 1961 The Beatles consolidated their position as the biggest band in Liverpool, frequently headlining shows with Rory Storm & The Hurricanes (pictured below) and their friend Ringo Starr. And when Pete Best was ill and missed a gig it was Ringo who stood in. Beyond Merseyside, however, they were still unknown, as they found out when they travelled south to play Aldershot Palais on 9 December. The gig had not been advertised and no tickets sold. A trawl of the local bars and the promise of a free show lured 18 people to the gig.

November: Brian Epstein Meets The Beatles

On 9 November the elegantly-suited Brian Epstein joined the hordes at the Cavern Club to see one of The Beatles' regular lunch-time shows. As manager of the record department at the nearby Whitechapel branch of his father's chain of NEMS electrical appliance stores, he was already aware of The Beatles, having had to track down the Tony Sheridan & The Beat Brothers' 'My Bonnie' single for eager fans. He also wrote a record review column for *Mersey Beat* magazine that devoted considerable space to the band. He was introduced to the band afterwards but it was a month before he came up with a management proposal, promising to get them a record contract. 'We were in a daydream before Brian came along,' John Lennon said. 'He was trying to clean our image up. He'd tell us that jeans were not smart and could we possibly wear proper trousers. But he let us have our own sense of individuality. We stopped chomping on cheese rolls and jam butties on stage. And we smartened up.'

1962

January: The Decca Audition

Using his contacts as a record shop manager, Brian Epstein approached Decca Records and, after A&R manager Mike Smith had seen The Beatles at the Cavern, they were asked to audition in London on 1 January 1962. The band endured a 10-hour drive down on New Year's Eve in stormy conditions and the following morning played a one-hour set consisting of 15 songs chosen by Epstein, including three of their own: 'Like Dreamers Do', 'Hello Little Girl' and 'Love Of The Loved'. They were competent but nervous and Decca opted for another group, Brian Poole & The Tremeloes. The head of A&R Dick Rowe memorably told Epstein, 'Guitar groups are on their way out'.

April: Stuart Sutcliffe's Death

The Beatles were feeling flush enough to fly to Hamburg on 13 April to start a 48-night run at the Star Club. But any delusions of grandeur were immediately wiped out on arrival when they were met by Astrid Kirchherr who told them that Stuart Sutcliffe had died of a brain haemorrhage just three days earlier. He had been suffering from blinding headaches and a post-mortem showed that the untreated head injury he'd suffered in a fight after a show nearly two years earlier was probably responsible.

May: EMI Record Deal

The gloom of The Beatles' third trip to Hamburg in the wake of Stuart Sutcliffe's death was lifted on 9 May when they received a telegram from Brian Epstein saying, 'Congratulations boys. EMI request recording session. Please rehearse new material.' After a dispiriting and fruitless trek around other record companies, Epstein had been introduced to George Martin (pictured on the right), head of A&R at Parlophone Records, an EMI subsidiary label. Martin listened to the Decca audition tapes and unusually offered Epstein a contract, subject to a recording test. On 6 June, four days after returning from Hamburg, The Beatles made their first visit to EMI's Abbey Road studios where they played a selection of material and cut four demos: 'Besame Mucho', 'Ask Me Why', 'Love Me Do' and 'P.S. I Love You'.

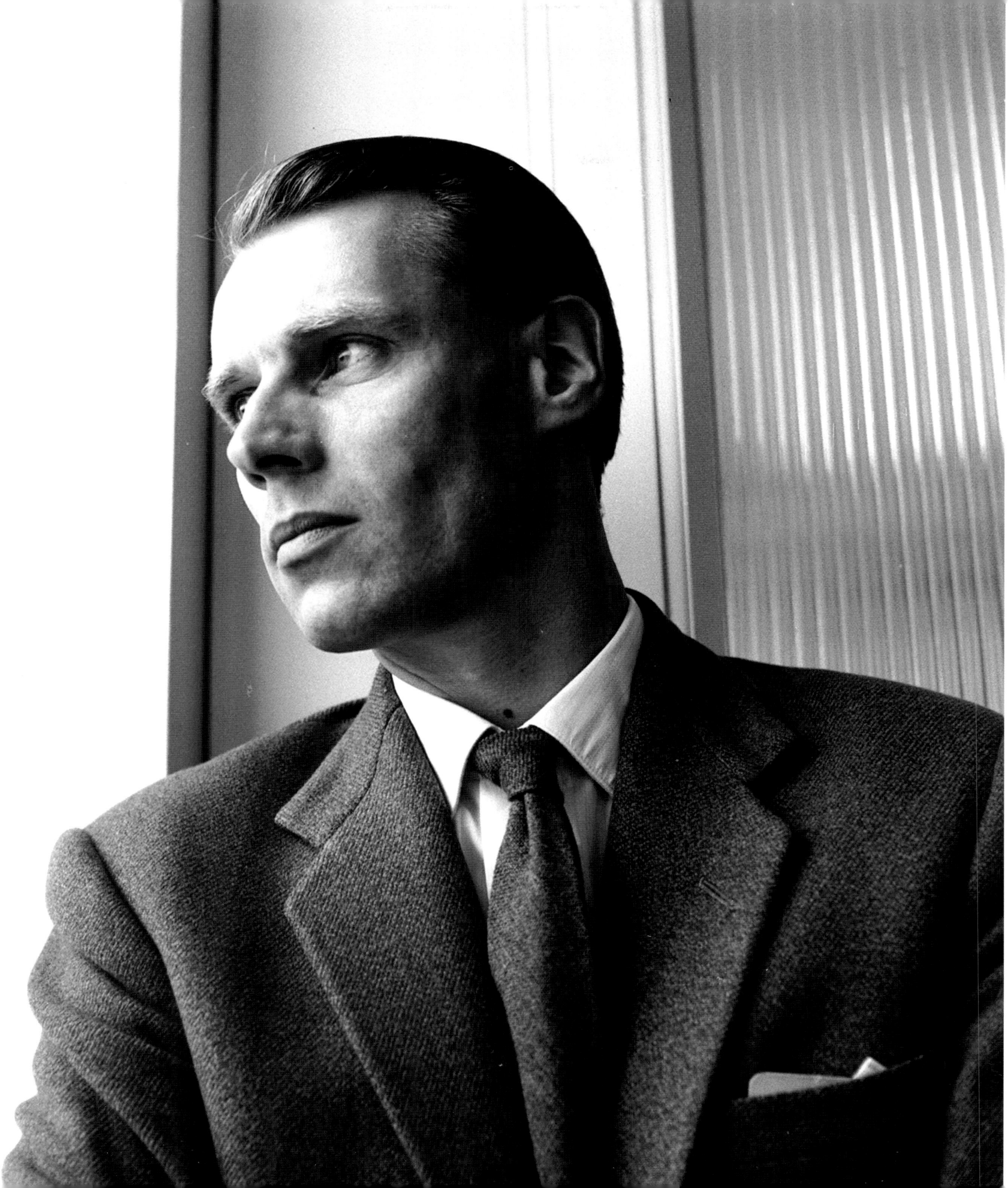

August: Ringo Joins The Beatles

After the first session George Martin told Brian Epstein that he would be using a session drummer for their recordings as he wasn't sure Pete Best could cut it in the studio. This brought a simmering discontent with Best to a head. It wasn't just the mop-top hairstyle he refused to wear; he didn't seem to fit in with the other three. The problem was, Best was a very popular member of The Beatles among their fans. Nevertheless the others told Epstein to fire Best and hire Ringo. Many Beatle fans were indeed angered by the news and Ringo's first gig with the band two days later on 18 August at the Cavern ended in fights and George Harrison received a black eye.

August: John Marries Cynthia Powell

On 23 August, with the furore of Pete Best's sacking still raging, John Lennon married his pregnant girlfriend Cynthia Powell in a five-minute ceremony at Liverpool's Mount Pleasant Registry Office. Lennon's aunt Mimi pointedly refused to attend and Cynthia was given away by her brother. Paul McCartney was best man and afterwards Brian Epstein took them all to lunch at a local café which unfortunately did not serve alcohol. Epstein had lent the couple his city centre bachelor pad but Lennon spent his wedding night on stage at Chester Riverpark Ballroom.

October: 'Love Me Do'

The choice of The Beatles' first single was a source of contention between the band and producer George Martin. The band argued strongly for 'Love Me Do' and Martin agreed it was the best of their songs, but he wasn't entirely convinced and gave them a demo of a Mitch Murray ballad, 'How Do You Do It?', to learn. The group rearranged the song in their own style and recorded it, along with 'Love Me Do', at their second Abbey Road session on 4 September. But it lacked the conviction of 'Love Me Do' and Martin was swayed. He was also not yet convinced by new drummer Ringo Starr and hired session drummer Andy White when the band returned to record the song again a week later. Ringo was given a tambourine to bang. 'Love Me Do', released on 26 October, reached No. 17 in the chart with Epstein himself rumoured to have ordered 10,000 copies. 'How Do You Do It?' later became a No. 1 hit for Gerry & The Pacemakers, who stuck to The Beatles' rearrangement.

November & December: Last Hamburg Trips

The Beatles made two more visits to Hamburg in November and December, honouring commitments made earlier in the year. It was a distraction the band could have done without as their 'Love Me Do' single was moving their career in a different direction. Their attempts to 'make show' for the German punters sometimes reached demented proportions; at one show John Lennon appeared on stage clad in his underpants and a toilet seat round his neck. It was perhaps a fitting last gasp of the first Beatles era.

The Beatlemania Era: 1963-65

1963-65

Between early 1963 and early 1964 The Beatles went from being virtual unknowns to international pop superstars, a position they maintained over the next two years by an intense schedule of recording and touring, as well as two major feature films. They did it by writing consistently better and better songs, often under extreme pressure, and by charming the media who seized on the group's popular appeal and turned it into Beatlemania.

There were other factors that helped to drive The Beatles' success. Britain shivered under a blanket of snow for the first three months of 1963 and the news was dominated by the Profumo scandal and its political fall-out. The newspapers needed a feel-good story and The Beatles provided it. Their mop-top haircuts were a newspaper layout artist's dream and their witty, intelligent and lively attitude to journalists ensured a stream of positive stories.

Similarly, America was traumatized by President Kennedy's assassination in November 1963. Two months later The Beatles were a sensation before they'd even set foot in the country. When they did the sensation exploded as the media revelled in their repartee: 'How did you find America?' 'Just turn left at Greenland' (John Lennon). 'What do you call that hairstyle?' 'Arthur' (George Harrison).

Manager Brian Epstein's role in The Beatles' success cannot be overemphasized. He made them presentable, he oversaw their UK career and planned their American breakthrough meticulously. They were the first British group to crack America, changing the whole course of popular music as they did so.

1963

January: 'Please Please Me'

'Gentlemen, you have just recorded your first number one,' producer George Martin told The Beatles after they'd completed 'Please Please Me'. He was right … just. It was released on 11 January, the same day that The Beatles appeared on the influential *Thank Your Lucky Stars* networked ITV show. The single made the Top 20 at the start of February and, although it peaked at No. 2 in the most important Record Retailer chart, five other charts placed it at No. 1. Not everyone liked it, though. Jimmy Saville on Radio Luxembourg said 'I hope it pleases somebody. It's a terrible noise.'

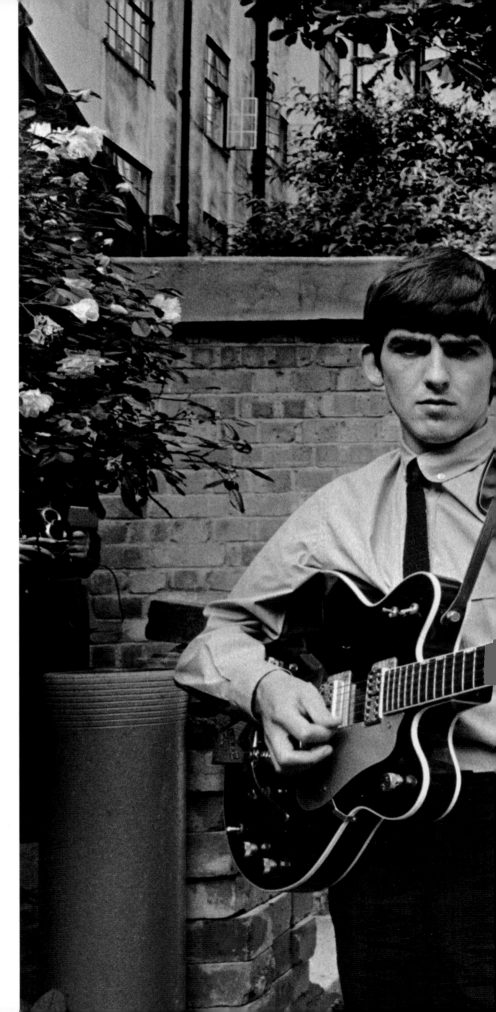

February: First UK Tour

When 'Please Please Me' hit No. 1, The Beatles were on their first UK package tour, bottom of a bill topped by child singing star Helen Shapiro. Eager to please, Lennon and McCartney had even written a song for her, 'Misery', but Helen's management never showed it to her. By the end of the tour they were closing the first half of the show. On their second tour they 'supported' American stars Chris Montez and Tommy Rowe but closed the show after the second date. It was the same situation on their third tour when Roy Orbison wisely decided not to follow them. By then, getting The Beatles in and out of the theatre each night had become a major operation.

March: Please Please Me

The 10 songs needed to complete the first Beatles album were recorded in one 13-hour session on 11 February. George Martin was looking to capture the atmosphere of their Cavern set in the studio. Paul McCartney: 'We came into the studio at 10 in the morning, did one number, had a cup of tea, relaxed, did the next one, a couple of overdubs. And by about 10 o'clock that night we'd done 10 songs and we just reeled out of the studio,

John clutching his throat tablets.' He needed them after the hoarse yells on the final 'Twist And Shout'. Released on 22 March, *Please Please Me* went to No. 1 in April and stayed there until it was replaced by *With The Beatles* in November.

52

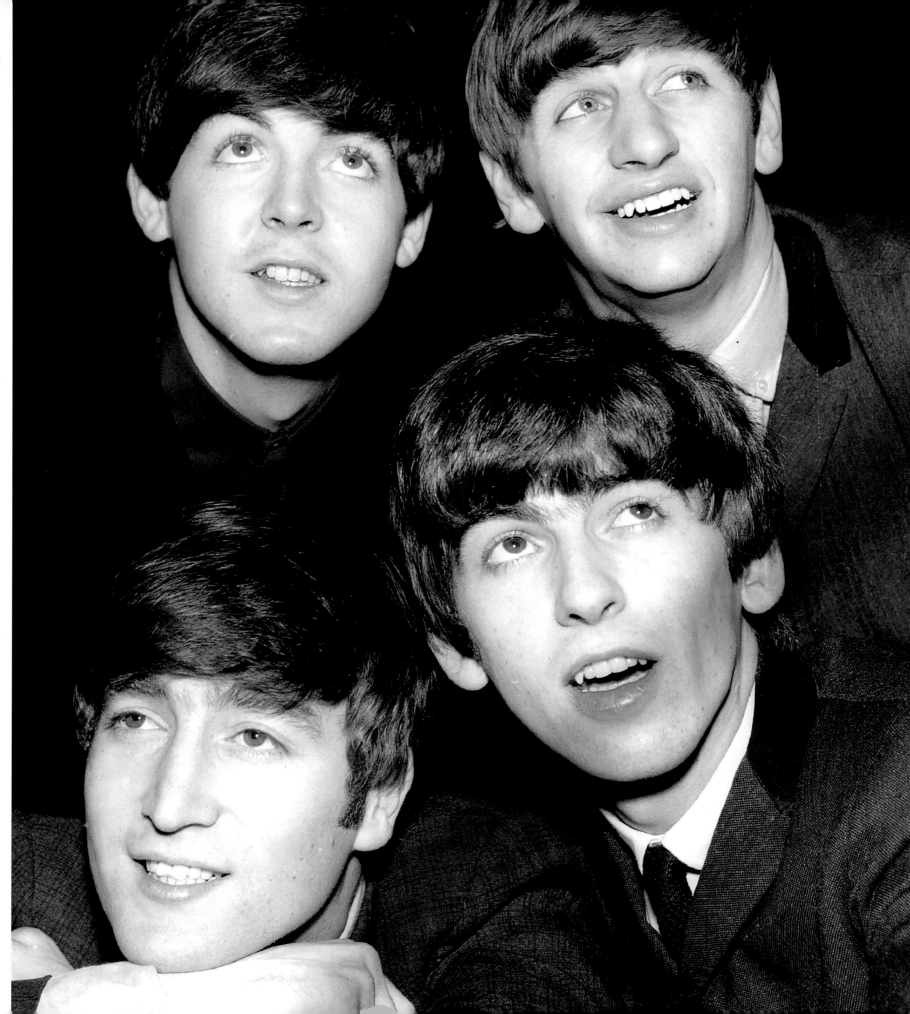

April: 'From Me To You'

Written on the Helen Shapiro tour bus travelling between York and Shrewsbury, 'From Me To You' was accepted rather than seized upon by George Martin for The Beatles' third single. He shouldn't have worried. Released on 11 April, it spent seven weeks at No. 1. John Lennon: 'Paul and I had decided not to do anything too complicated. That's why we always included words like "me" and "you" in the titles. It helps listeners identify with the lyrics.'

April: Lennon And Epstein's 'Affair'

On a hastily arranged break at the end of April, Brian Epstein and John Lennon flew to Torremolinos, Spain, without Cynthia and baby Julian whom Lennon had scarcely seen. Lennon: 'The rumours went around that he and I were having a love affair. Well, it was almost a love affair but not quite, it was never consummated … It was my first relationship with someone I knew was a homosexual … We used to sit in a café looking at all the boys and I'd say "Do you like that one? Do you like this one?" I was rather enjoying the experience, thinking like a writer all the time, "I am experiencing this."' A couple of months later, at Paul McCartney's twenty-first birthday party in Liverpool, Cavern Club DJ Bob Wooler teased Lennon about the trip and was beaten up by Lennon.

May: Beatles At The BBC

As the only national radio and TV broadcaster in the UK, the BBC was vital for getting exposure for The Beatles. After one guest appearance to promote 'Please Please Me' on the Light Programme's *Saturday Club* (with an audience of around 10 million) in January 1963, the band's radio-friendly charm and fast-working professional attitude saw them invited back nine more times and appear on other shows like *Easy Beat* and *Side By Side*. In May they were given their own Tuesday teatime show, *Pop Go The Beatles*. Their first BBC television spot was in April on the *625 Show*, followed by a children's TV appearance on *Pops & Lenny*, singing 'Please Please Me' with the popular glove puppet. In June John Lennon joined the panel of the Beeb's flagship TV pop show, *Juke Box Jury*, but in an unaccustomed display of public grumpiness he voted every record a miss.

August: Final Cavern Show

John Lennon: 'We couldn't say it but we didn't really like going back to Liverpool. Being local heroes made us nervous. We felt embarrassed in our suits. We were worried that our friends might think we'd sold out. Which we had in a way.' The Beatles had also outgrown their Merseyside haunts. They played their last Cavern Club show on 3 August and John Lennon had the sleeve of his mohair jacket ripped off trying to get in. The group spent that summer on the traditional showbiz seaside circuit, playing four or five nights apiece at Great Yarmouth, Margate, Blackpool, Rhyl, Weston-Super-Mare, Llandudno, Bournemouth and Southport.

August: 'She Loves You'

'She Loves You' confirmed The Beatles' phenomenon. Paul McCartney: 'I got the idea for doing one of those answer-type songs, where someone says "She loves you" and the other person goes "Yeah yeah yeah". But the idea of having the sixth chord at the finish was George Harrison's and George Martin said "That's very old-fashioned", and we said, "Yeah, but it's nice, isn't it?"' The gimmicky 'Whoooo' on the chorus with Lennon and McCartney shaking their mop tops together was another idea from the Helen Shapiro tour bus. With advance orders of 750,000, 'She Loves You' became the biggest selling single in Britain until 1978 when it was topped by Paul McCartney and Wings' 'Mull Of Kintyre'.

October: Sunday Night At The London Palladium

The country's most-watched TV entertainment show, ITV's *Sunday Night At The London Palladium*, booked The Beatles as the headline act on 13 October. They opened the show with a brief, tantalizing appearance and, after their specially rehearsed four-song set, they joined the other guests on the show's famous roundabout for the closing credits. The next day's papers reported the crowd scenes outside the theatre with unusual gusto, even though the same scene was being played out across the country night after night.

October: Tour of Sweden

The Beatles' first foreign tour since their Hamburg trips produced the same fan hysteria and mayhem they were getting in the UK, only more so. They arrived at Stockholm Airport to be greeted by mobs of screaming girls and the authorities struggled to control the chaos. The band played five concerts and recorded a live TV show, escorted everywhere by the police, who even stood guard outside their hotel rooms. But it didn't stop the girls from getting in or the band from partying. They arrived back at Heathrow Airport a week later to another sea of screaming fans. Passing through the airport at the time was the presenter of the top-rated US TV weekly entertainment show, Ed Sullivan, who wondered what all the fuss was about....

November: The Royal Command Performance

The British Establishment's acknowledgement that The Beatles had 'made it' came with a summons to appear at the annual Royal Command Performance on 4 November in front of the Queen Mother and Princess Margaret. They were not top of the bill although they were the most talked-about. And they charmed the toffs. McCartney introduced 'Till There Was You' as a song sung by Sophie Tucker, 'Our favourite American group'. And when it came to 'Twist And Shout' Lennon famously told the people in the cheap seats to 'clap your hands, the rest of you rattle your jewellery'.

November: Epstein Sets Up American Visit

No British act had ever cracked the American pop market and EMI's US subsidiary Capitol showed no interest in releasing 'Please Please Me', even after it was a British No. 1. It was released by the independent Vee Jay label in the summer of 1963 but made no impression. Neither did 'From Me To You', and 'She Loves You' also failed when it was issued on Swan Records. In November, Brian Epstein flew to New York and eventually persuaded Capitol executives to release the next Beatles single, 'I Want To Hold Your Hand', in January. Epstein also met top TV presenter Ed Sullivan, who had already witnessed Beatlemania at first hand, and set up two appearances on *The Ed Sullivan Show* in February.

November: With The Beatles

Released on 22 November, The Beatles' second album was a major leap forward, from the songs and production to the stylish black and white cover. There were seven new Lennon and McCartney songs, notably the opening trio of 'It Won't Be Long', 'All I Got To Do' and 'All My Loving', plus George Harrison's first Beatles song, 'Don't Bother Me'. The six covers included three from the little-known Tamla Motown label ('Please Mr Postman', 'You Really Got A Hold On Me' and 'Money'), preparing the British pop audience for the Motown sound. The album replaced *Please Please Me*, which had been No. 1 for 30 weeks, and kept The Beatles at the top of the UK album charts for a further 21 weeks.

November: 'I Want To Hold Your Hand'

The first worldwide hit for The Beatles started in the basement of Paul McCartney's girlfriend Jane Asher's central London house where he and John Lennon were trying to write a mock-gospel song. What emerged was an original, memorable single full of subtle tricks, from the deliberate stumble on the opening riff to the clever hand-clapping and the harmony crashes on the chorus. With UK advance orders of a million they could have recited the telephone directory and got to No. 1. But they were still trying harder. Every single was a significant improvement on the last.

December–January 1964:
The Beatles' Christmas Shows

After a six-week all-conquering tour of Britain, The Beatles rounded off 1963 with their own Christmas Show at London's Finsbury Park Astoria: 16 nights, two shows a night. Between spots by Cilla Black and The Fourmost (both managed by Brian Epstein and his fast-growing NEMS Agency), The Beatles acted in sketches that were embarrassingly poor, even by the low standards of English pantomime. The leaden scripts offered no chance for their spontaneous ad libs. Not that it damaged their artistic credibility. A *Sunday Times* critic declared they were 'the greatest composers since Beethoven'.

December–January 1964:
American Breakthrough

America got its first sight of The Beatles on 10 December when CBS News broadcast a piece on the 'Beatles phenomenon' that was gripping the quaint old UK, including some concert footage featuring screaming fans. A couple of days later a listener wrote to Washington DC's WWDC Radio asking to hear 'I Want To Hold Your Hand'. A DJ got his airline stewardess girlfriend to bring over a copy from London and played it. The station switchboard was immediately swamped with requests to hear it again. The DJ told a friend in Chicago where the same thing happened. And again in St Louis, and then all over the country. Just before Christmas, Capitol increased the advance pressing order for the single from 200,000 to a million and rush-released it on Boxing Day, thereby giving kids a whole week to hear it on radio and buy it before going back to school. By which time the pressing order had run out.

1964

January: First US No. 1

When 'I Want To Hold Your Hand' shot to No. 1 in the *Cashbox* chart on 18 January, having leapt from No. 43 to the top slot, The Beatles were in Paris on a three-week run at the Olympia, staying at the grandiose George V Hotel where they were also writing songs for their forthcoming feature film. A telegram from Capitol Records announcing the triumph was initially greeted with stunned silence and disbelief … and then a party that started with a pillow fight and got a lot wilder. The impeccably attired Brian Epstein even allowed himself to be photographed with a chamber pot on his head. Paul McCartney: 'We didn't come down for a week.'

February: Arrival In New York

Pan Am flight 101 to New York carrying The Beatles and their entourage, including Cynthia Lennon making her first 'official' engagement as John's wife, left Heathrow Airport on 7 February with radio stations across America broadcasting regular bulletins on its progress. When they emerged from the plane at JFK Airport they were greeted by 5,000 fans, 200 journalists waiting to ask questions and a group of photographers dangling off a fork-lift truck. At the Plaza Hotel they were trapped on the twelfth floor listening to non-stop Beatles music on their transistor radios and watching their arrival on TV. Later, Paul McCartney slipped out to the Playboy Club while Ringo and Mr and Mrs Lennon were taken to the Peppermint Lounge which was not the 'Home of the Twist' as they'd been promised but home to a Beatles tribute band.

February: The Ed Sullivan Show

The Beatles' first appearance on *The Ed Sullivan Show* on 9 February was a defining moment in American rock'n'roll history. It drew a TV audience of over 70 million, including Alice Cooper, Billy Joel, Joey Ramone, Tom Petty and Joe Walsh who have all remembered how it changed their lives. The 'Fab Four' opened the show with 'All My Loving', 'Till There Was You' and 'She Loves You', returning later to play 'I Saw Her Standing There' and 'I Want To Hold Your Hand'. They didn't close the show, though. That honour went to 'acrobatic physical comedy' act Wells & The Four Fays.

February: First American Concerts

Between their two *Ed Sullivan* shows, The Beatles played their first American concerts, at the 10,000 capacity Washington Coliseum and the prestigious New York Carnegie Hall. The only sour note of their US visit came when they attended a reception at the British Embassy in Washington and were jostled boorishly by Embassy staff for autographs. One woman even tried to cut off a lock of Ringo's hair.

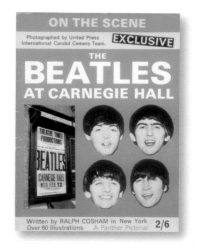

February: American Hits Pile Up

The success of 'I Want To Hold Your Hand', selling five million copies during its seven-week stay at No. 1, provoked a feeding frenzy among the labels that had previously released Beatles singles without success. Swan Records reissued 'She Loves You' that promptly went to No. 1 for two weeks. And Vee Jay re-released 'Please Please Me' that got to No. 3. Before long there was a free-for-all as almost every track The Beatles had recorded for their first album, that was itself re-packed into two different versions, was issued as a single while writs flew back and forth as Capitol frantically sought to regain control of The Beatles' catalogue.

March: 'Can't Buy Me Love'

Immediately after The Beatles returned from America they completed work on their next single that had been written and recorded in Paris at the start of the year. George Martin's suggestion of adapting the chorus to start and finish the song paid dividends. Paul McCartney: '(It was) my attempt to write in a bluesy mode. The idea behind it was that all these material possessions are all very well but they won't buy me what I really want. It was a very hooky song.' Advance orders ensured that the single was instantly No. 1 in the UK and US. From now on every new Beatles single went to No. 1 – everywhere.

March & April:
Filming Begins On A Hard Day's Night

With the script and shooting schedule barely in place, The Beatles started work on their first feature film, an inside slant on Beatlemania. Director Richard Lester: 'It was all a bit of a blur. We only had seven weeks' shooting. Nobody really had any time to stop and think over what they were doing. But the incredible speed with which it was made worked to its benefit'. Fortunately the band had already written and recorded a batch of songs for the soundtrack. The film's title came from a remark Ringo made on location late one evening.

April: US Chart Domination

The *Billboard* US singles chart for 4 April showed The Beatles occupying the Top Five positions with 'Can't Buy Me Love' followed by 'Twist And Shout', 'She Loves You', 'I Want To Hold Your Hand' and 'Please Please Me' – a feat that is unlikely ever to be equalled. In addition there were seven other Beatles singles in the Top 100. The following week there were two more entries. Between 22 February and 25 April The Beatles monopolized the top two positions in the chart.

April: In His Own Write

John Lennon was the first Beatle to undertake a solo project when he published a book of his writings and drawings titled *In His Own Write*. It featured Lennon's free-form linguistic style and impressed *The Times Literary Supplement* who said, 'Worth the attention of anyone who fears for the impoverishment of the English language and the British imagination'. Or as Lennon himself put it: 'As far as I'm conceived this correction of short writty is the most wonderfoul lark I've ever ready.'

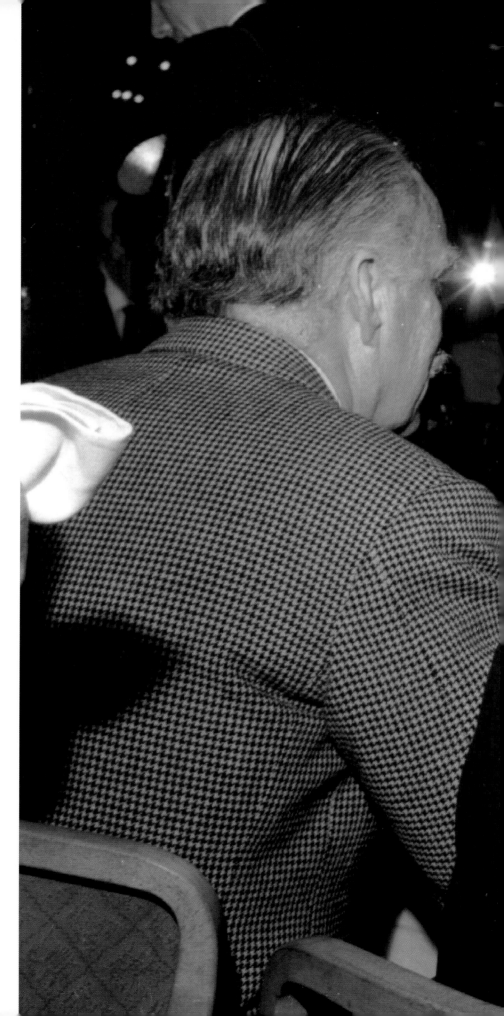

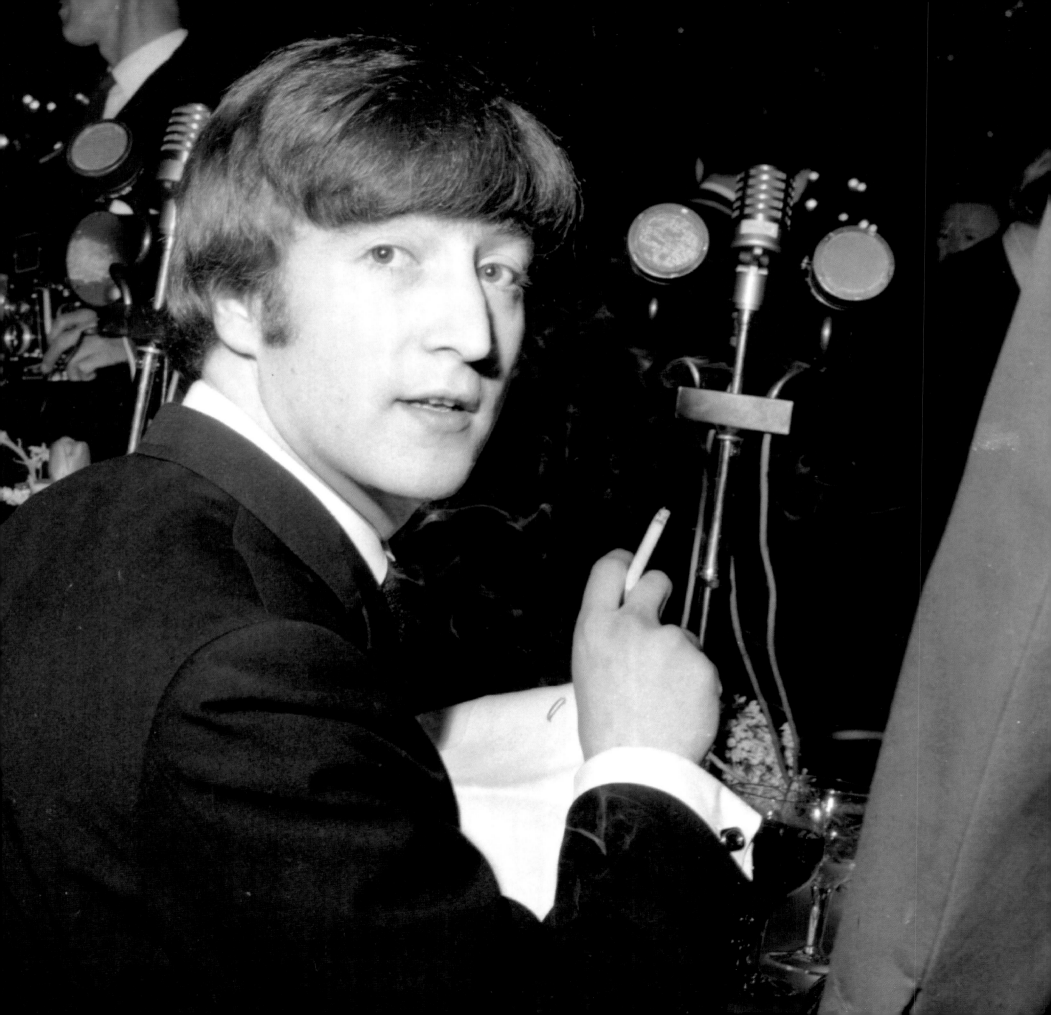

June: Ringo's Collapse

The Beatles' world tour got off to a bad start when Ringo collapsed during a photo shoot the day before they left for Denmark and was diagnosed with tonsillitis and pharyngitis, requiring rest and quiet. On George Martin's recommendation the group hired 24-year old session drummer Jimmy Nicol (pictured on the far left) as a temporary replacement, although George Harrison at first refused to play without Ringo. Jimmy Nicol: 'I was having a bit of a lie-down after lunch when the phone rang. It was EMI asking if I could come down to the studio to rehearse with The Beatles. Two hours after I got home I was told to pack my bags for Denmark.'

June: Hong Kong And Australia

Temporary drummer Jimmy Nicol played his first concert with The Beatles the day after joining them in Copenhagen. In Holland the following day, a TV appearance ended in chaos after fans engulfed the stage and the band had to calm their nerves in Amsterdam's red-light district. In Hong Kong they failed to sell out two shows, mainly because the promoter was charging the average weekly wage for a ticket. In Adelaide, Australia, an estimated 200,000 people lined the route from the airport to the City Hall where the mayor presented the Beatles with toy koala bears. In Melbourne, where Ringo finally caught up with the tour, a civic reception ended in a melee when dignitaries and fans scrambled to touch the band. It was cold and pouring with rain in Sydney but they were still paraded round the streets in an open-top bus. In Brisbane a group of Beatles-haters pelted the group with eggs during their open-top ride and again at their concert.

July: A Hard Day's Night

The Beatles' third album saw them on the upswing, with 13 Lennon and McCartney songs written under pressure, all good, some great, like the title track. As George Martin said, 'You only have to hear one chord to recognize it'. There's a more overtly romantic, almost sentimental, tone to many songs and the sound is subtly enhanced by George Harrison's newly acquired 12-string Rickenbacker. In America, as with all their early releases, Capitol Records made two albums out of it by repackaging, renaming and adding singles and B-sides left off the UK release.

July: A Hard Day's Night Premiere

The police closed Piccadilly Circus for the London premiere of *A Hard Day's Night* at the London Pavilion on 6 July, keeping at bay a 12,000 crowd who'd come to see The Beatles getting

in and out of their cars. And the critics raved, even the ones from the 'quality papers' who'd been expecting the usual B-movie standard from rock stars. The band were more apprehensive about the Liverpool premiere five days later as they'd barely been back since moving to London. But they needn't have worried; nearly 200,000 turned out to

watch them en route to the Town Hall for a civic reception. Paul McCartney's day was made when he spotted his old English teacher in the crowd.

August-September: First American Tour

The itinerary alone of the first Beatles tour of America was madness: 32 shows in 24 cities in 34 days. The mayhem that surrounded their every move from plane to hotel to gig and back again was constant. It started when they arrived in San Francisco for the first concert and were driven 50 yards to a fenced enclosure where photographers were waiting inside and 9,000 fans outside. They escaped seconds before the fences collapsed.

In Kansas City their bed linen was cut into three-inch squares and sold for $10 apiece. It was the same with their towels at the Hollywood Bowl. Much of the time the band did not know where they were. Most of the time they were playing with

shoddy equipment, although no-one could hear. They baulked only when disabled people were brought into their dressing room to be 'cured'. The only moment of light relief came when Bob Dylan came to visit them in New York and turned them on to marijuana.

October–November: UK Tour

The schedule for The Beatles' only British tour of 1964 was almost as manic as the American tour: 54 shows in 25 cities in 33 days. And if the concerts were smaller, the same cinemas and theatres they'd been playing a year earlier, and the crowd numbers proportionally less, the strain of constant isolation was the same. And at every opportunity they'd have to dash back to London for recording sessions for their next album.

September: Jelly Babies

Early on in The Beatles' career, in one of the thousands of articles that were being written about them, George Harrison happened to mention that jelly babies were his favourite sweet. As a result Beatles concerts were generally performed in a hail of jelly babies hurled by hysterical fans. This was unpleasant but at least the jelly babies were soft and squashy. In America jelly babies didn't exist so fans switched to jelly beans that were sugar-coated and harder. And they hurt.

November: 'I Feel Fine'

Like 'A Hard Day's Night', 'I Feel Fine' was instantly recognizable from the first note, in this case an acoustic guitar string distorted by feedback. George Martin: 'People thought the feedback was an accident. It wasn't. John and Paul spent a lot of time trying to get that sound'. It was Lennon's song but George Harrison carried it with a fiendishly difficult riff and a guitar solo that was ahead of its time. McCartney supplied the rhythmic rocker 'She's A Woman' on the B-side.

December: Ringo's Tonsils Removed

On 1 December Ringo checked into London's University College Hospital to have his tonsils removed. The press reported that he brought red pyjamas, a pink toothbrush and an unnamed science fiction thriller. He also had a record player delivered to his room. A dedicated phone line was set up with a recorded message on his progress. Two fans who had hoped to buy the tonsils were left disappointed however. Ringo: 'Nobody is getting my tonsils as a souvenir. Believe me, I will burn them'.

December: Beatles For Sale

Beatles For Sale was the group's third album in a year, not to mention all the singles and EPs, and the strain began to show. They even looked a little weary on the cover. Many of the eight new Lennon & McCartney songs were downbeat in tone including the opening 'No Reply', 'I'm A Loser' and 'Baby's In Black', although they roused themselves on 'Eight Days A Week' and the chirpy ballad 'I'll Follow The Sun'. And the six covers harked back to their Cavern Club days rather than following up their interest in the Tamla Motown sound.

December–January 1965:
More Beatles Christmas Shows

At the end of a tumultuous year The Beatles came down to earth and returned to panto with their second season of 20 Christmas Shows, this time at London's Hammersmith Odeon. The scripts were marginally better: one sketch had the Fab Four dressed

as Arctic explorers looking for the Abominable Snowman. The support acts included Elkie Brooks, Freddie & The Dreamers and The Yardbirds. John Lennon supplied the drawing for the front and back cover of the programme, thus making it an instant collectors' item.

1965

February: Ringo Marries Maureen Cox

On 11 February a tonsil-less Ringo married Maureen Cox, the Liverpool girlfriend he'd been 'going steady' with since the Cavern Club days, at London's Caxton Hall Registry Office. The ceremony was attended by Mr and Mrs Lennon and George Harrison who quipped, 'Two down and two to go'. Paul McCartney was on holiday in Tunisia. The newlyweds drove to Hove for their honeymoon but were almost immediately discovered by fans and returned to London.

February: Work Begins On Help!

After the phenomenal success of *A Hard Day's Night*, the budget for the second Beatles movie was doubled to £500,000 and Richard Lester retained as director. Producer Walter Shenson promised a 'mad, zany comedy thriller' but they started with another threadbare plot that amounted to little more than Ringo being kidnapped by a weird cult. And the locations were mainly determined by accountants who were looking for ways to offset the massive tax bill the band were facing, hence Barbados and Switzerland. John Lennon: 'It was a drag because we didn't know what was happening. In fact Richard Lester was a bit ahead of his time … but we were all on pot by then and the best stuff was on the cutting room floor, with us breaking up and falling all over the floor.' For some time the film was going to be called *Eight Arms To Hold You* but that was never a title that was going to inspire a great Lennon and McCartney song.

March: The Beatles' First Acid Trip

John Lennon: 'A dentist in London laid it [acid] on George, me and the wives, without telling us, at a dinner party at his house … He said "I advise you not to leave" and we all thought he was trying to keep us for an orgy in the house and we didn't want to know'. Cynthia Lennon: 'We got away somehow in George's Mini but he came after us in a taxi. It was like having the devil follow us in a taxi … Everybody seemed to be going mad … Pattie [Boyd, George Harrison's girlfriend] wanted to get out and smash all the windows along Regent Street. Then we turned round and started heading for George's place in Esher. God knows how we got there'. John Lennon: 'God, it was just terrifying but it was fantastic. George's house seemed to be like a big submarine and I was driving it….'

April: 'Ticket To Ride'

Lennon and McCartney's most ambitious song to date, 'Ticket To Ride' kept The Beatles well ahead of the growing pack behind them, The Rolling Stones, The Who, The Kinks and The Small Faces, as the 'Swinging London' scene gathered momentum. The song's subtle rhythm was anchored by Ringo's skilful drumming and the charm and gusto of the harmonies helped to disguise Lennon's misogynist lyrics. The B-side, 'Yes It Is', was a harmony-drenched remake of an earlier B-side, 'This Boy', with George Harrison using his latest gizmo, a volume/tone pedal.

June: The Beatles' MBE

The decision by Prime Minister Harold Wilson, who was also Member of Parliament for the Liverpool constituency of Huyton, to include The Beatles in the MBE honours list for the Queen to approve predictably drew howls of outrage from many previous recipients. Among them was a Mr Hector Dupuis (who'd received his award for his services to the Canadian armed services recruitment agency) who complained that he'd been put on the 'same level as vulgar nincompoops'. It took George Harrison to point out that MBE actually stood for 'Mr Brian Epstein' which showed that The Beatles knew where their true allegiances lay.

July: Help! Premiere

For the second time in a year, Piccadilly Circus was closed for another Beatles movie premiere on 29 July at the London Pavilion. This time the critics were not so kind. The spontaneity that had characterized *A Hard Day's Night* was notably absent and after some fine visual gags: the evil cult leader throwing darts at a film of The Beatles playing, the band's bachelor pad

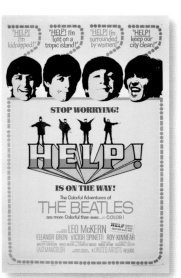

behind a terrace house façade, the film fell increasingly flat. One unexpected bonus came when George Harrison's ears pricked up at the sound of an Indian band hired to play in a restaurant during filming.

August: Help!

Help! was the last straightforward album The Beatles made. The song quality was still there, particularly on the title track, 'You've Got To Hide Your Love Away', 'Ticket To Ride' and of course 'Yesterday'. But the enthusiasm for the format was waning. After releasing five albums in less than two and a half years (nine in America), The Beatles were tiring of writing songs to order. John Lennon later said that the album's title track was a cry for help. 'It was my fat Elvis period. I was fat and very depressed.'

August–September: Second American Tour

Starting at New York's Shea Stadium in front of an estimated 56,000 fans, The Beatles' second American tour consisted of 12 concerts in 10 cities. It was shorter than their first tour but more intense because they were playing stadiums and the mayhem surrounding them was incessant. The only respite, apart from a refreshing visit by Bob Dylan in New York, was a five-day break in Beverley Hills where they partied with The Byrds and paid a visit to Elvis Presley that was embarrassingly stilted at first but loosened up once the guitars came out. Paul McCartney: 'He had the first remote switcher for a television I'd ever seen. He was switching channels and we were like, "How are you doing that?"'

September: 'Yesterday'

Paul McCartney had written the melody to 'Yesterday' early in 1965. 'I had a piano by my bedside and I must have dreamed it because I tumbled out of bed and put my hands on the piano keys and I had a tune in my head. It came too easy. In fact I didn't believe I'd written it. I thought maybe I'd heard it before. I went round for weeks playing the song to people asking them "Is this like something? I think I've written it." And people would say "No, it's not like anything else. But it's good."' For a while the song was known as 'Scrambled Eggs' until the lyrics came together. George Martin: 'It wasn't a three-guitar-and-drums kind of song. I said "What about a string accompaniment?" Paul said "Yuk. I don't want any of that Mantovani rubbish." Then I thought back to my classical days and said, "Well, what about a string quartet then?"'

September: The Beatles Cartoon Series

Scarcely had the hysteria over The Beatles' second US tour died down than the first episode of *The Beatles* cartoon series was aired on ABC in the States. The band were depicted in their early mop-top days circa *A Hard Day's Night* as each animated sequence led up to a Beatles song. The band themselves had nothing to do with the cartoon and their voices were dubbed by actors. By the time the series ended in 1967 (it was never shown in the UK), The Beatles looked nothing like their cartoon characters, but that didn't stop the endless repeats that even John Lennon found amusing to watch when he relocated to New York in the 1970s.

December: Rubber Soul

The Beatles crossed the watershed with *Rubber Soul*, recorded in the autumn of 1965. John Lennon: 'We were just getting better technically and musically, that's all. Finally we took over in the studio. We were learning the technique on *Rubber Soul*. We were more precise about making the album.' As the group took control, producer George Martin's role changed but remained vital, translating their musical thoughts and ideas into studio reality. His baroque piano solo on 'In My Life' was a masterpiece. The songs started getting personal, notably John Lennon's 'Norwegian Wood' and 'Nowhere Man', and George Harrison proved that he could now compete with Lennon and McCartney on 'If I Needed Someone'. The new attitude was summed up on the opening 'Drive My Car' with its complex chord changes, lyrical black humour and strident guitar.

December:
'We Can Work It Out' / 'Day Tripper'

The first ever double A-sided single. Both songs were recorded quickly – within a day – and while 'Day Tripper', based on a Lennon guitar riff, was initially serviced to radio as the 'preferred' song, DJs quickly preferred the quirkier 'We Can Work It Out' with its one-note harmonium drone and sudden switch to waltz time on the chorus. A film of The Beatles lip-synching the song was made for television and can fairly claim to be the world's first pop video.

December: John's Father Freddie

John Lennon had never seen his father, Freddie, until he resurfaced and released a single at the end of 1965 entitled 'That's My Life (My Love And My Home)'. Lennon: 'I opened the *Daily Express* and there he was, washing dishes in a small hotel near where I was living. I didn't want to see him. I was too upset about what he'd done to me and my mother. But he sort of blackmailed me in the press. I fell for it and we had some kind of relationship.' Freddie Lennon died a few years later of cancer but not before marrying a secretary who had worked for The Beatles and fathering a child.

1966-68

The first cracks in the seemingly impregnable façade that had been built up by three years of Beatlemania seemed insignificant. When John Lennon casually remarked that The Beatles were 'more popular than Jesus' in March 1966 he had no idea that his words would haunt him with increasing malevolence for the rest of the year. The Beatles narrowly avoided another major furore when the infamous American 'Butcher' album was withdrawn just as it was about to go on sale.

But there was no way out of the touring nightmare which spiralled towards terror until, after a third American tour, they decided to stop. Henceforth they would be a studio band. At first this was no problem. *Revolver* (1966) and *Sgt. Pepper's Lonely Hearts Club Band* (1967) were incandescent albums, the best The Beatles ever made. But manager Brian Epstein's death in August 1967 was the turning point. As Lennon said, 'I thought, "We've f***ing had it."' The idea that The Beatles could manage themselves was preposterous. Their next project, *Magical Mystery Tour* (1967), was a total shambles. Apple Corps, naively described by Paul McCartney as 'A kind of Western communism' was even worse.

For a while they continued to act collectively, travelling to India together to raise their consciousness. And they delivered two anthems that rocked the world in 1967 and 1968: 'All You Need Is Love' and 'Hey Jude'. But the arrival of Yoko Ono at John's side ripped apart the last ties that bound them together. There was little sign of collaboration on *The Beatles* at the end of 1968.

1966

January: George Marries Pattie Boyd

George Harrison married model Pattie Boyd at Epsom registry office on 21 January. They had been going out together since meeting on the set of *A Hard Day's Night* nearly two years earlier. Paul McCartney was the best man. John Lennon and Ringo were both on holiday with their wives, planned as a decoy for the media, although there were dozens of photographers waiting for the happy couple after the ceremony. The bride was dressed by Mary Quant. The honeymoon was in Barbados.

February: Bernard Webb

Paul McCartney: 'I tried to write a song under another name, just to see if it was the Lennon/McCartney bit that sold our songs.' He chose pop duo Peter & Gordon (pictured below). Peter Asher was girlfriend Jane's brother, for whom he'd already written a couple of hits and wrote 'Woman' under the name of Bernard Webb. The single reached No. 83 in the US and No. 47 in the UK before the ruse was rumbled and Mr Webb's real identity was confirmed. The single eventually reached No. 14 in the US and No. 28 in the UK.

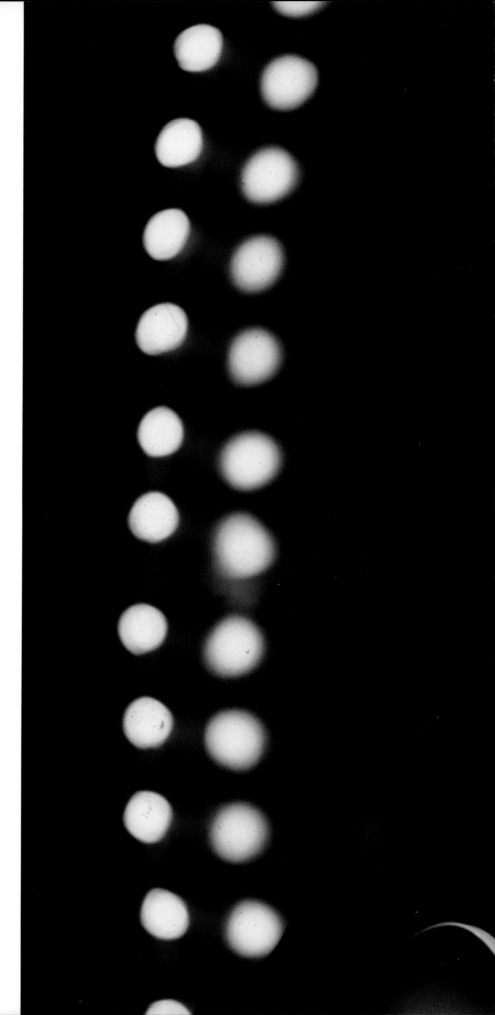

March: 'More Popular Than Jesus'

In an interview with 'trusted' journalist Maureen Cleave in the London *Evening Standard* John Lennon, talking about religion, remarked that The Beatles were 'more popular than Jesus now'. The comment aroused no interest in Britain, but when it was reprinted in America a few days later there was instant outrage among Christian groups in the Midwest and South. Radio stations started banning Beatle records and the same fans who had been buying them by the million were now exhorted to destroy them. The Ku Klux Klan ceremonially nailed a Beatles record to a cross and burnt it. In South Africa the apartheid regime banned the state broadcasting company from playing Beatles records. The ban lasted beyond The Beatles' break-up to include John Lennon solo records, although records by Paul McCartney, George Harrison and Ringo Starr were permitted.

May: Final UK Concert

The Beatles' appearance at the *NME* Poll Winners Concert at Wembley Empire Pool on 1 May was their final public concert in the UK. They topped a bill that featured The Rolling Stones, Cliff Richard & The Shadows, The Small Faces, Dusty Springfield, The Who, Roy Orbison and The Walker Brothers. The Beatles' 15-minute set featured 'I Feel Fine', 'Nowhere Man', 'Day Tripper', 'If I Needed Someone' and 'I'm Down'. Tickets for the North Upper Tier were 25 shillings (£1.25p).

May: 'Paperback Writer' / 'Rain'

Two contrasting songs heralded the next phase of The Beatles' recording career. The sprightly, commercial 'Paperback Writer' was written by Paul McCartney in response to his aunt Lil who was tired of all his love songs. 'Rain' was John Lennon's first foray into psychedelia, complete with a backwards tape layered on at the end, an effect he discovered at home late one night when he wrongly threaded a tape spool. But it was McCartney who suggested slowing down the whole backing track to enhance the droning effect.

May: Promo Pioneers

In late 1965 The Beatles had filmed mimed performances of 'Day Tripper' and 'We Can Work It Out' for use on TV shows. For 'Paperback Writer' and 'Rain' the band shot two films on location at Chiswick House, London, with director Michael Lindsay-Hogg (who would later film *Let It Be*) using rhythmic editing, slow motion, hand-held camera shots and little attempt to mime the songs. These were the forerunner of the pop video.

June: The 'Butcher' Cover

When photographer and Salvador Dalí fan Robert Whitaker handed The Beatles white coats, slabs of meat and dismembered dolls as props the band happily played along. John Lennon: 'It was inspired by our boredom and resentment at having to do another photo session and another Beatle thing. We were sick to death of it.' The band selected one of the shots for the US-only album *Yesterday And Today*. Astonishingly, no alarm bells rang at Capitol Records until a few promotional copies were sent to radio DJs and store managers, most of whom reacted with horror. Capitol frantically recalled all 750,000 copies of the album from the distribution depots and glued a hastily prepared alternate sleeve onto the cover. A few of the original covers survived and became highly-prized collector's items. In 2005 a shrink-wrapped, unopened 'Butcher' album sold for $39,000.

June & July: Final World Tour

The first leg of what would be the last Beatles tour in Germany included a concert in Hamburg which they had not revisited since 1962. In Japan they faced protests from right-wing groups for playing at Tokyo's Budokan, a shrine to the nation's war dead, and an estimated 30,000 uniformed men lined the route from their hotel, in which they remained trapped for four days. It all turned nasty in the Philippines, ruled by President Marcos, where they were effectively kidnapped by the militia who boarded the plane and 'escorted' them to various functions and parties before they eventually reached their hotel at 4 am. Next morning they slept in, unaware that the president's wife, Imelda Marcos, had organized a party for them to meet the sons and daughters of senior military officers. That afternoon they played two stadium shows for 80,000 fans without incident but the following morning they awoke to find no room service and no security. They faced a harrowing journey to the airport where they were spat at and jostled. Their plane was unable to leave until various trumped-up charges were settled, at the expense of their concert fees.

August: Revolver

Released on 5 August, *Revolver* marked the emergence of The Beatles as a studio band. They brought their individual songs into the studio, the assembly point for their combined influences. Lennon and McCartney's songwriting was diverging: McCartney was heading deeper into melody and soul with 'Here There And Everywhere', 'For No One' and 'Got To Get You Into My Life' while Lennon was heading deeper into his own head with 'She Said She Said', 'And Your Bird Can Sing' and 'Tomorrow Never Knows'. But that simply enriched the album's diversity. Harrison's writing blossomed with three songs including the opening 'Taxman' and his first sitar song 'Love You To'. Disciplined and timeless, *Revolver* is perhaps the ultimate Beatles album.

August: 'Yellow Submarine' / 'Eleanor Rigby'

Two tracks from the *Revolver* album were released simultaneously as a double-A-sided single. Ringo semi-yodelled his way through the kiddie-friendly 'Yellow Submarine' while John Lennon clanged bells, blew bubbles in a bucket and strutted round like a demented sailor. 'Eleanor Rigby' was another shaft of Paul McCartney brilliance, a wistful lament for loneliness enhanced by George Martin's arrangements for double string quartet. It won the 1966 US Grammy Award for Best Contemporary Vocal Performance, only their second Grammy despite 16 previous nominations.

August: John's Public Apology

When The Beatles arrived in America for their third tour, teenagers were still making bonfires of Beatle records and fundamentalist Christian preachers were still condemning John Lennon's 'More popular than Jesus' remark that had been taken out of context and was now widely misquoted as 'Bigger than Jesus'. Brian Epstein convened a special press conference in New York to clarify Lennon's remarks but the media were not appeased. Lennon was forced to make a public apology for any offence caused at another press conference in Chicago.

August: Third US Tour

With the smell of burning vinyl still lingering over The Beatles, their third tour was a tense, nerve-laden trek across 14 cities, trapped in hotels by death threats as well as fans. Everything came to a head in Memphis. During the concert someone let off a firecracker and the band were all visibly shaken. Afterwards they came to a collective decision: this would be the last tour. Several stadium shows failed to sell out, although the screaming and the shoddy sound equipment still rendered the band largely inaudible. Those who enjoyed listening to The Beatles perhaps preferred doing so at home.

August: Last Public Concert

The Beatles' last public concert was at San Francisco's Candlestick Park on 29 August, a foggy, windy night. The 42,000-capacity stadium was less than two thirds full with ticket prices ranging from $4.50 to $6.50. The Beatles played 11 songs in just over half an hour behind a 2-m (6-ft) fence, ringed by police and security with an armoured car standing by, engine running. Ringo: 'It seemed that this could possibly be the last time but I never felt a hundred per cent certain until we got back to London. John wanted to give up more than the others, He said that he'd had enough.' George Harrison: 'Before one of the last numbers we set up this camera … on the amplifier and Ringo came off the drums and we stood with our backs to the audience and posed for a photograph because we knew that was the last show.'

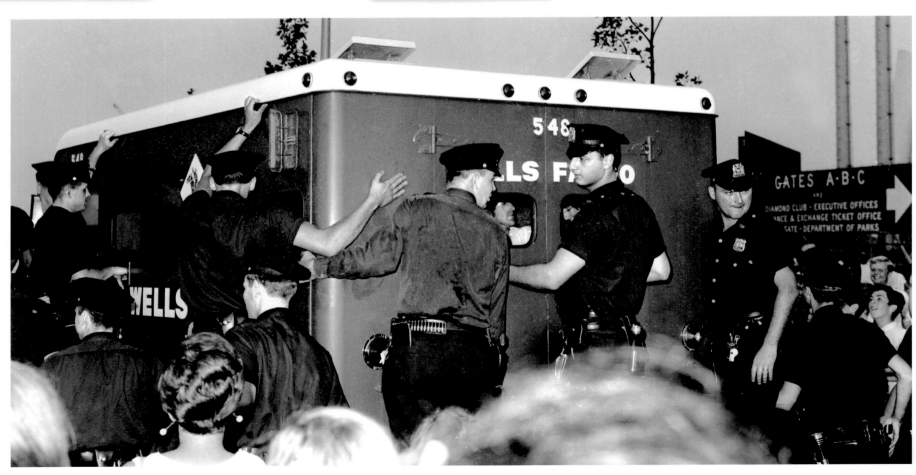

September–November: A Short Hiatus

Less than three weeks after the last Beatles concert, John Lennon was in Spain filming *How I Won The War*, a surreal anti-war movie directed by Richard Lester. 'The Beatles had stopped touring and I thought that if I stopped and thought about it I was going to have a big bum trip for nine months.' Paul McCartney busied himself writing the score for another film, *The Family Way* (arranged by George Martin), and then holidayed in France and Africa. Ringo managed to hook up with both of them along the way. George Harrison headed to India where he spent five weeks studying with sitar player Ravi Shankar.

November: Sgt. Pepper Sessions Begin

When news that The Beatles would no longer play concerts was publicly confirmed in November, there was considerable speculation over the band's future. *The Sunday Times* even ran a 'Beatles split' story, complete with analysis and obituary. Even The Beatles were unsure how the band could continue simply as a recording group. But when they reconvened at Abbey Road Studios in November there was plenty of material for them to work on. They spent most of the next five months in the studio. Significantly, they had also dropped their mop-top image and started displaying their own individual dress sense, just as the British fashion industry was moving into 'Swinging London' overdrive.

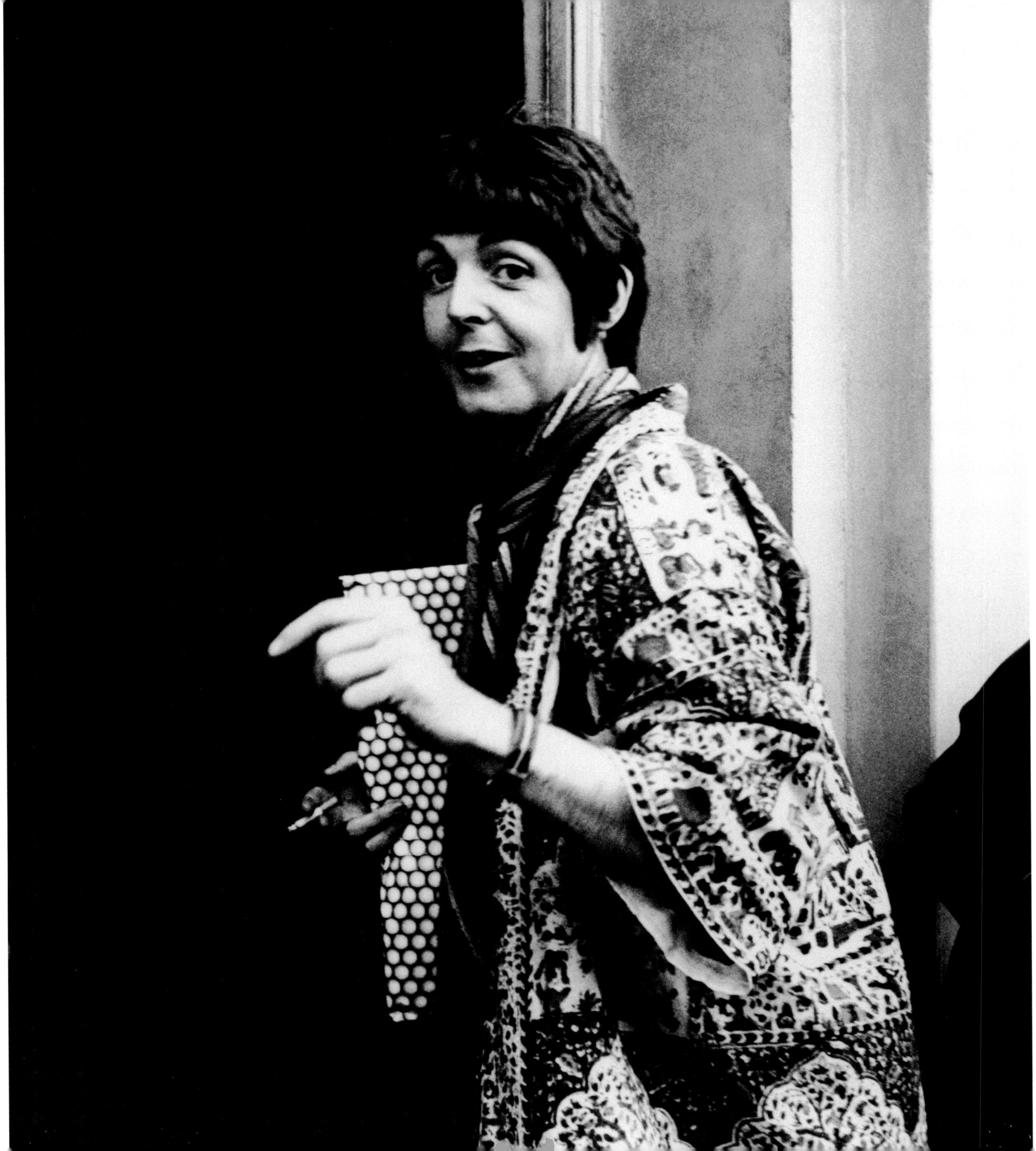

1967

February:
'Penny Lane' / 'Strawberry Fields Forever'

The first record to emerge from the studio-bound Beatles was another pair of contrasting McCartney and Lennon songs, a recurring feature of recent singles but, with time to perfect and polish, the songs had moved up another level. Both made a nostalgic return to Liverpool for their inspiration but while McCartney strode gaily down Penny Lane 'beneath the blue suburban skies', nodding at the people and shops he remembered, Lennon slunk back to the overgrown grounds of Strawberry Field (a now-demolished children's home) where he used to play, creating a sound collage of rampaging strings and trumpets, heavy insistent drumming, trippy lyrics, mysterious mutterings, fade-outs, fade-ins and, of course, backwards tapes. It was the first Beatles single not to make No. 1 in the UK since 'Love Me Do', held off the top spot by Engelbert Humperdinck's 'Release Me'. Curiously, the band didn't seem bothered.

April: Beatles Reject Movie Script

Several ideas for a third movie had been considered by The Beatles: an adaptation of *The Three Musketeers*, even *The Lord Of The Rings*, but none had gone beyond the discussion stage. Paul McCartney was a fan of maverick playwright Joe Orton (he'd invested £1,000 in his play *Loot*) and in January 1967 Orton was commissioned to write a script that became *Up Against It*. The plot featured four characters representing different aspects of one person but it also involved murder, adultery, political chicanery and cross dressing, ending up with all four characters sharing one woman. Not surprisingly, The Beatles rejected the script. Paul McCartney: 'We didn't do it because it was gay. We weren't gay and really that's all there was to it.'

June: Sgt. Pepper's Lonely Hearts Club Band

Sgt. Pepper's Lonely Hearts Club Band was the sound of The Beatles walking on water. No other album reflected and defined its time better. It was the soundtrack for 1967's 'Summer Of Love', endlessly replayed as the newly-christened flower children lapped up every trick and nuance and then went looking for more. And there were plenty, from the eager anticipation of an audience at the start to the final babble on the run-out groove. It was Paul McCartney's master stroke to give The Beatles an alter ego to play with. And the segues that linked each song (there were no bands separating the tracks) meant that each side of the album had to be played in its entirety. This did not prevent the BBC from banning 'A Day In The Life' and 'Lucy In The Sky With Diamonds' for perceived drug references.

June: The Sgt. Pepper Cover

The cover of *Sgt. Pepper's Lonely Hearts Club Band* was as groundbreaking as the contents. Designed by British 'pop' artist Peter Blake it depicted The Beatles as the Sgt. Pepper band in military-style, day-glo satin costumes, surrounded by life-size cutouts of 70 or so of their heroes, as well as waxwork models (borrowed from Madame Tussauds) of The Beatles in their mop-top days. Among those who failed to make the cut were Jesus, Gandhi and Hitler. The band's name was spelt out in a floral display in the foreground and the flower-delivery boy was allowed to create a guitar out of yellow hyacinths.

June: McCartney Admits Drugs Use

The cover feature on The Beatles in *Life* magazine on 16 June included an interview with Paul McCartney in which he admitted taking LSD. He was promptly besieged by the media. Three days later he gave an interview to ITN who broadcast it on the *Nine-O'Clock News*. He stated that he was simply being honest and suggested that the media was responsible for spreading the story. The incident came as a series of high-profile drug busts were taking place. The following month *The Times* ran a full-page advertisement calling for the decriminalization of cannabis, signed by 65 prominent people including Nobel scientist Francis Crick, novelist Graham Greene and all four Beatles.

June: Appearance on BBC's Our World

BBC TV devised *Our World* as the first live television satellite linkup involving 14 countries from five continents and a potential audience of some 400 million. The Beatles were chosen to represent the UK and wrote 'All You Need Is Love' for the occasion. They were beamed around the world from the Abbey Road Studios with a 13-piece orchestra and a host of friends on backing vocals including Mick Jagger, Keith Richards, Marianne Faithfull, Eric Clapton and Keith Moon, surrounded by flowers, balloons and placards that translated 'All you need is love' into different languages. The single was released the following month and went to No. 1 in at least 14 countries.

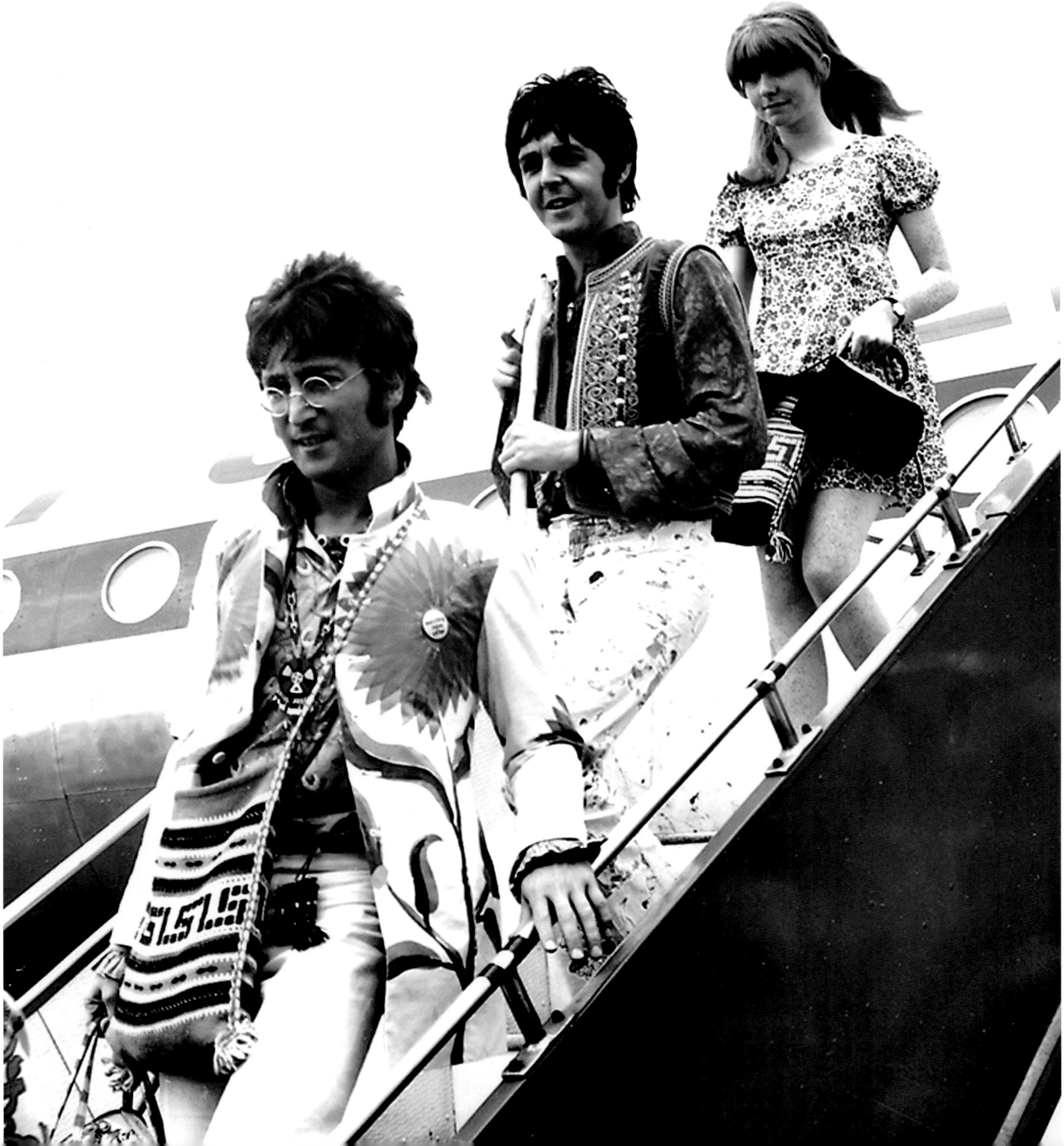

July: Aegean Trip

Encouraged by John Lennon's new Greek friend 'Magic' Alex, The Beatles and entourage flew to Greece, interested in buying an island in the Aegean where they could live, record and make merry in the sunshine. It was a chaotic trip with missing yachts, broken-down hire cars and the media anticipating The Beatles' every move. But the island that had been selected for them seemed suitable and Harrison, Lennon and McCartney (Ringo had returned to look after his heavily pregnant wife) made plans for a recording studio, meditation posts and a go-kart track. Back home, the management was instructed to arrange for a currency export licence, but by the time the formalities had been completed the idea had been abandoned.

August: The Maharishi Mahesh Yogi

It was Pattie Harrison who told The Beatles about transcendental meditation and persuaded them to come to a lecture by Indian spiritual guru the Maharishi Mahesh Yogi in London on 24 August. They were so impressed that they immediately volunteered to attend the Maharishi's weekend seminar in Bangor, travelling with him, Mick Jagger and Marianne Faithfull on the train from Paddington (apart from Cynthia Lennon who got trapped in a fan scrimmage and missed the train). The seminar was held in a teacher-training college and The Beatles found themselves billeted in spartan student rooms alongside the Maharishi's followers and several intrepid journalists.

August: Brian Epstein's Death

The Beatles' manager Brian Epstein was found dead at his London home on 27 August. He was 32. A post-mortem revealed that he died from an overdose of sleeping pills. Although he had been suffering from depression, all the evidence pointed to an accidental overdose which was the verdict reached at the inquest. The Beatles, still in Bangor with the Maharishi, were barely able to comprehend the news in their transcendentally meditative state. Before they returned to London the Maharishi told them that Epstein's death in the physical world was 'not important'.

September:
Magical Mystery Tour Filming Begins

Having decided to manage themselves in the wake of Brian Epstein's death, The Beatles also decided to make their own movie. Paul McCartney had come up with the idea of a magical mystery tour and at short notice a coach was hired and painted in psychedelic patterns, a cast and crew assembled, and on 11 September the entourage drove to Teignmouth, Devon. There was no script, just an assortment of ideas and sketches. Like the itinerary, the filming was spontaneous and most of it was never used. The tour's progress was also slow as they were followed by a posse of journalists and sightseers and the coach had difficulty negotiating the narrow country lanes. Most of the scenes used in the film were shot later at West Malling airfield.

November: 'Hello Goodbye'

Somewhat inconsequential but insidiously addictive, 'Hello Goodbye' was written by Paul McCartney who claimed it was about duality, although the lyrics did not necessarily support this. Still, it gave The Beatles a Christmas No. 1 on both sides of the Atlantic. John Lennon's views on the song were unprintable, although this may have been because his own 'I Am The Walrus' was designated as a B-side instead of the double A-sided singles the band had been releasing of late. The promotional film for 'Hello Goodbye' was banned by the BBC because it broke Musicians' Union rules on miming.

November: Magical Mystery Tour Soundtrack

Recorded in the hazy afterglow of *Sgt. Pepper*, the songs on *Magical Mystery Tour* inevitably suffered in comparison, not because they were inferior but because they lacked focus and context. This was not helped in the UK where the six songs were released as a double EP with a gatefold sleeve encasing a booklet, a novel but disjointed format. For once the Americans

did it better: the US album put all the *Magical Mystery Tour* tracks on one side and filled the other with recent singles. The BBC censors clamped down again, banning John Lennon's dense epic 'I Am The Walrus' due to the word 'knickers'.

December: The Apple Boutique

Having set up Apple Corps to manage their affairs after Brian Epstein's death, The Beatles' first business venture was the Apple Boutique that opened in London's Baker Street on 4 December. Supposedly a shop where everything in it was for sale, it was essentially a fashion store designed by and for the 'beautiful people'. The exterior of the Georgian townhouse was given a psychedelic makeover with a brightly coloured mural. The venture was a financial disaster. Staff seemed reluctant to accept payment, and customers often didn't bother to trouble them. The boutique closed suddenly eight months later, liquidating itself by giving away its remaining stock.

December: McCartney-Asher Engagement

Actress Jane Asher first met Paul McCartney in 1963 and started a relationship with him soon afterwards. Her brother Peter was one half of Peter & Gordon for whom McCartney wrote several hits. Their relationship survived the madness of Beatlemania and beyond while she steadfastly maintained her own career. When McCartney announced their engagement at Christmas 1967 the only surprise was that it had taken so long. Seven months later Asher unexpectedly announced during a BBC interview that McCartney had broken off the engagement and they were no longer together. She has not spoken about it since.

December: Magical Mystery Tour Premiere

The *Magical Mystery Tour* film was premiered on BBC TV on Boxing Day 1967 to an estimated audience of 15 million. It received a unanimous critical mauling, mainly concerning the incoherent plot. It didn't help that the film had been shot in colour (or what passed for colour at the time) but was broadcast in black and white. The critical reaction in the UK deterred US television companies from acquiring screening rights and the film's 52-minute length made it unsuitable for cinemas. It wasn't broadcast on US TV until the Eighties.

1968

February: Trip To Rishikesh

The Beatles resumed their acquaintance with the Maharishi in mid-February when they, their wives, girlfriends and business managers flew out to his ashram at Rishikesh where they attended his initiator training course. Among the other initiators were actress Mia Farrow, Beach Boy Mike Love and Donovan. Ringo returned to Britain after 10 days; McCartney followed a couple of weeks later but Harrison and Lennon stayed until mid-April. The real bonus for the group was the burst of songwriting that the visit inspired. Some 30 new songs were written, many of which appeared on their next album.

March: 'Lady Madonna'

Paul McCartney continued his de facto leadership of The Beatles with a sparkling Fats Domino-inspired boogie, playing the rollicking piano riff and singing through cupped hands at one point. The backing vocals on the chorus were among the most sublime they ever recorded. America was not so impressed with 'Lady Madonna's retro charms and it peaked at No. 4. But the British taste for nostalgia made it yet another No. 1.

May: Apple Corps Launched

Apple Corps, which had been running The Beatles' own affairs, was officially launched as a fully-fledged business operation with a fanfare of publicity in London and New York. The company's main division was Apple Records which would release all future Beatles records as well as newly signed artists like Mary Hopkin. Other divisions included Apple Publishing, Apple Films, Apple Electronics and Apple Retail. Paul McCartney described it as 'A kind of Western communism' and appealed for people to send in demo tapes. Thousands did but most of the tapes were never listened to. Those who came in person to the elegant Apple office in London's Savile Row with a specific project, or even a vague idea, were often more fortunate, receiving an instant 'grant' for further research. Most of them were never seen again.

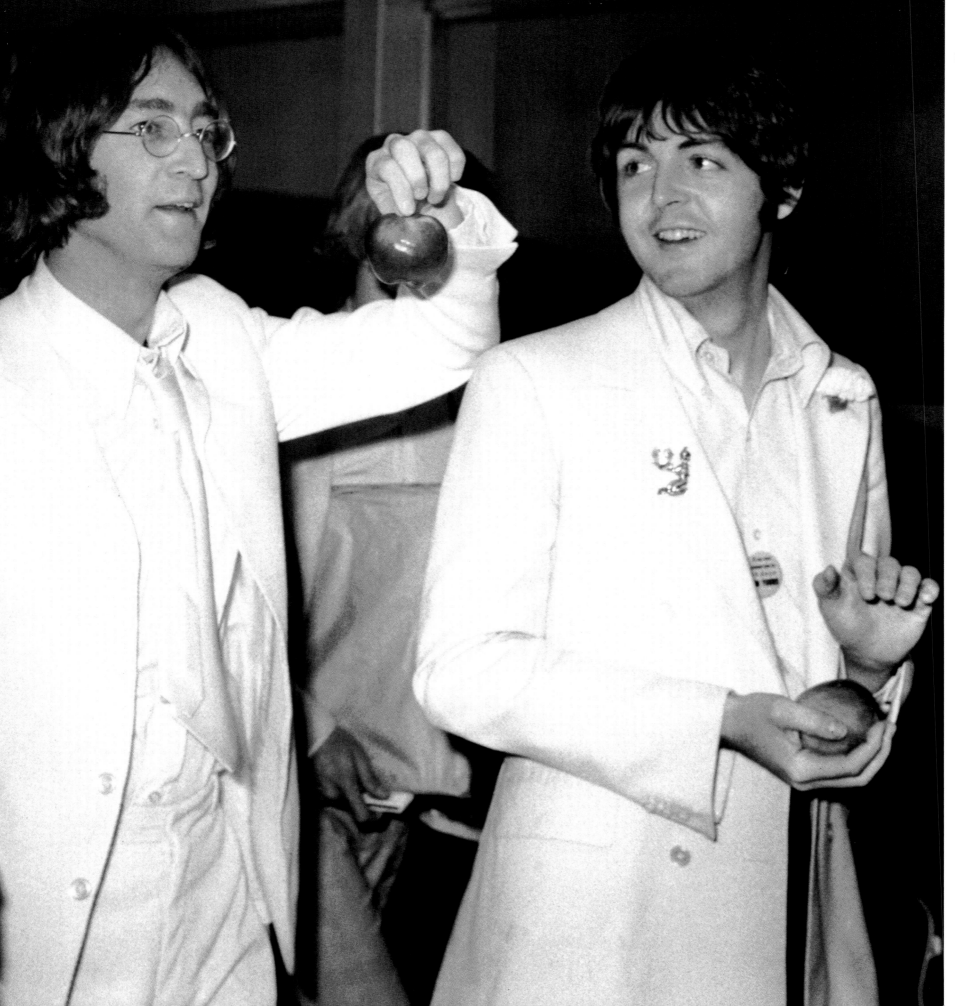

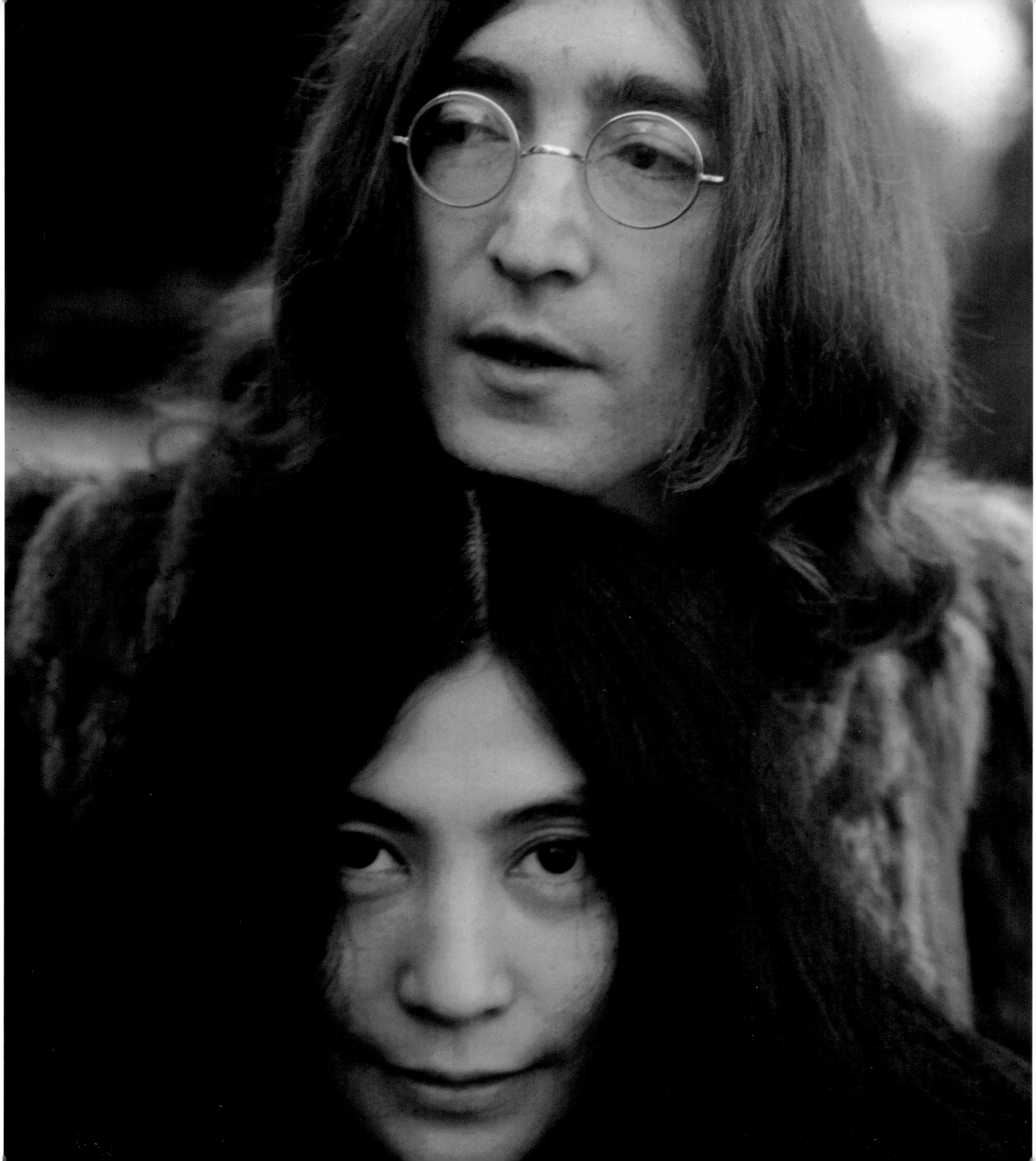

May: Yoko Ono

John Lennon first met Japanese avant-garde artist Yoko Ono in November 1966 at her exhibition, 'Unfinished Paintings And Objects'. 'There was an apple there on sale for £200. I thought it was fantastic. I got the humour in her work immediately.' He sponsored another exhibition and they remained in contact as he became increasingly intrigued by her radical approach to art. Lennon's marriage to Cynthia had wilted. 'It was just a normal marriage where nothing happens and which we continued to sustain.' They continued to go on holiday together and both travelled to India in early 1968. Lennon's confession of serial infidelity on the flight home shocked an unsuspecting Cynthia. In May, while Cynthia was away, Lennon invited Yoko over to listen to his tapes before they made one together. 'It was midnight when we started *Two Virgins* and it was dawn when we finished and then we made love at dawn. It was very beautiful.'

May: The Beatles Sessions

In late May The Beatles gathered at George Harrison's house to record a demo of all the songs they had prepared. It was immediately apparent that they had two albums worth of material to work on. Even Ringo had written a song. They started recording at Abbey Road a few days later with one significant difference: contravening the unwritten rule that wives and hangers-on were barred from the studio, Lennon arrived with Yoko who remained glued to his side. This did not improve the increasingly tense and strained relations within the group.

July: Yellow Submarine Premiere

The Beatles' ailing film career was revived by a project that they had almost nothing to do with. When the company that had made *The Beatles* cartoon series in 1965 got the rights to make a full-length animated cartoon the group showed little interest. The four new songs they were obliged to contribute were discards from the *Sgt. Pepper* and *Magical Mystery Tour* sessions. However, the animation was awash with psychedelic day-glo and, although the storyline, set in Pepperland, was weak, the cast of characters: Blue Meanies, Nowhere Men, Apple Bonkers and The Beatles themselves, had an irresistible charm for children of all ages.

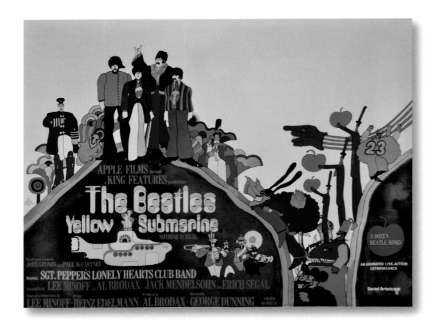

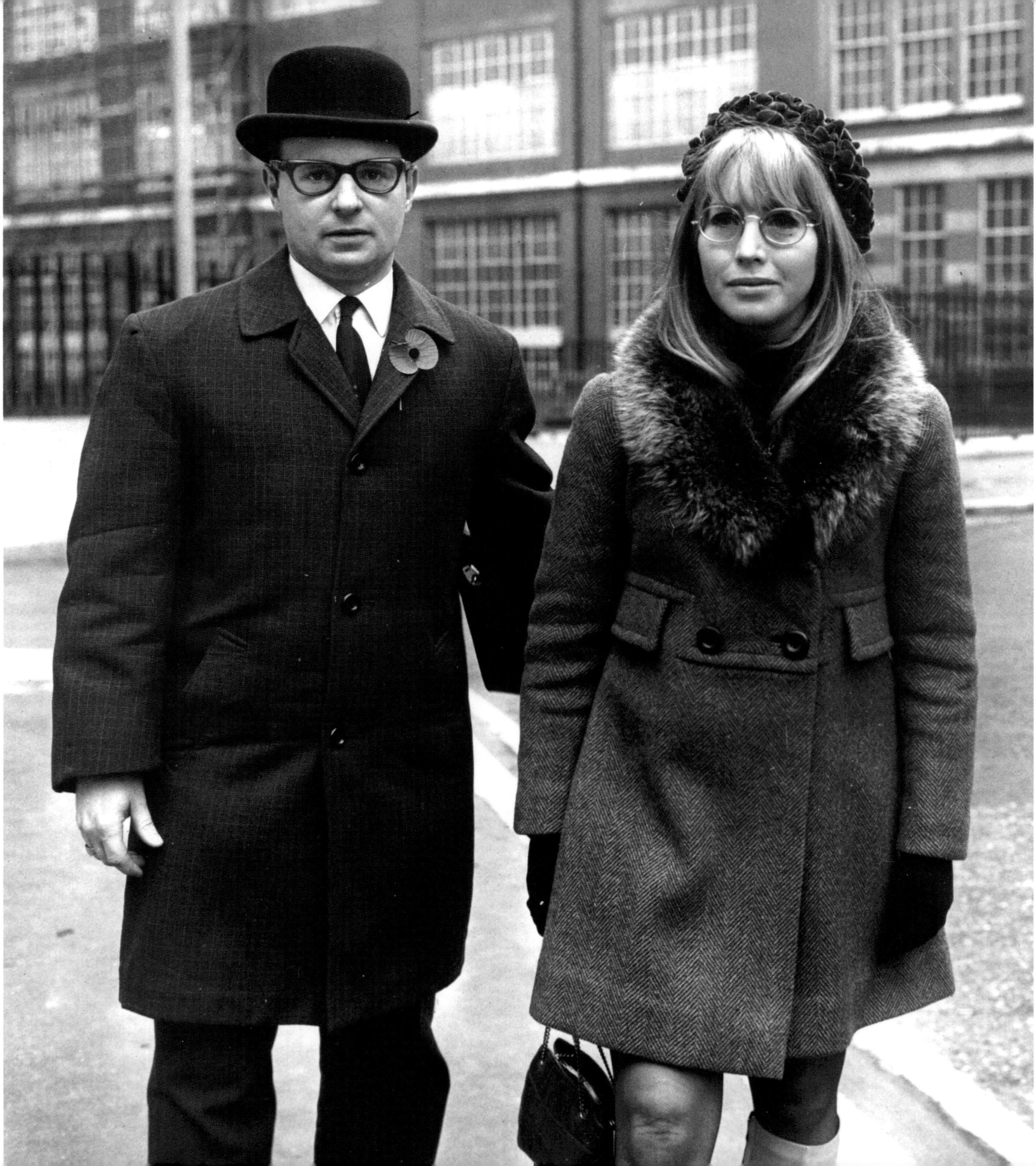

August: Cynthia Files For Divorce

John Lennon and Yoko Ono made their first public appearance as a couple at the opening night of *The John Lennon Play: In His Own Write* at London's Old Vic Theatre on 18 June, greeted by photographers who cried. 'Where's your wife?' Lennon wanted a divorce but did not want to be the guilty party. That changed when Yoko became pregnant. Cynthia was granted a decree nisi in November on the grounds of Lennon's adultery and was granted custody of their son Julian.

August: 'Hey Jude'

The Beatles' first release on Apple was their biggest-ever selling single. Written by McCartney on his way to see Cynthia and Julian Lennon (the only one of The Beatles to show support during her divorce), it was just a couple of verses, a middle section and a hefty fade-out. But it was heard as a communal anthem of hope with no political connotations, building from a simple beginning to a big orchestral finale. Worldwide sales topped eight million. Fortunately the BBC couldn't hear Lennon's four-letter contribution buried deep in the mix, otherwise they would have had to ban it.

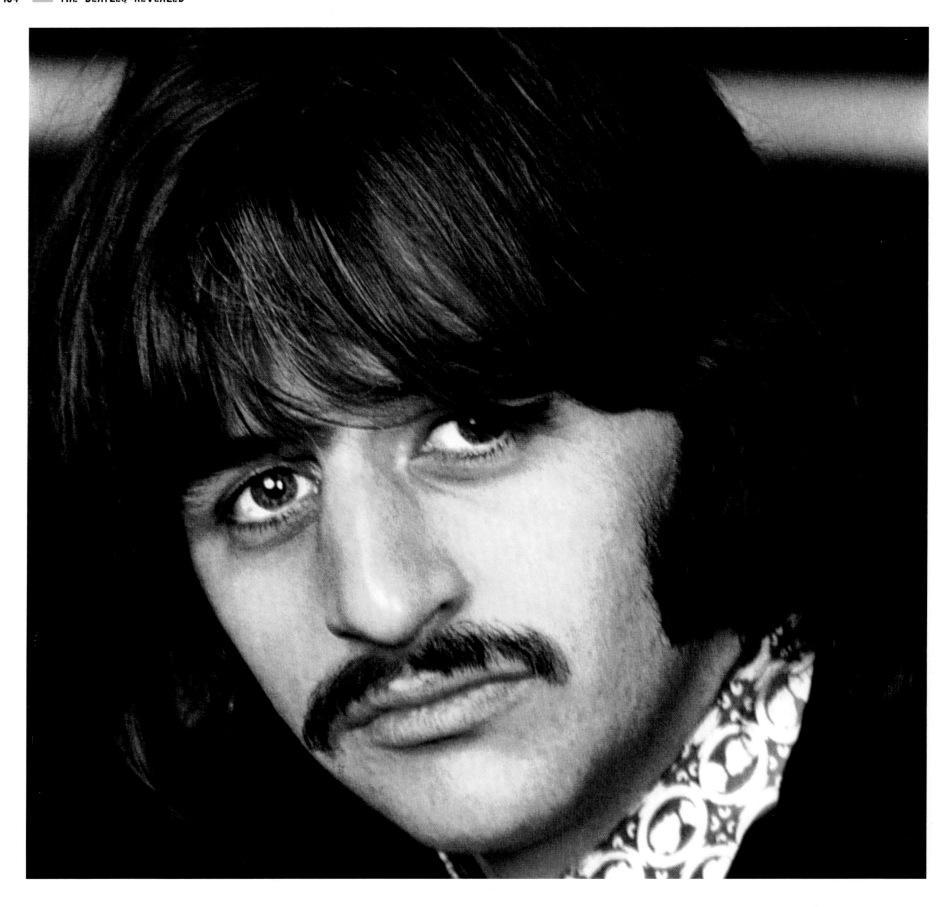

August: Ringo Quits (For Two Weeks)

The growing tensions in the studio as the band recorded their next album produced an unexpected twist when Ringo, the mildest and most easy-going of The Beatles, suddenly downed sticks and walked out. Ostensibly the reason was his dissatisfaction with his drumming. 'I knew we were all in a messed-up state. It wasn't just me; the whole thing was going down. There was no magic and the relationships were terrible.' Ringo flew to the Mediterranean and stayed on Peter Sellers' yacht, writing 'Octopus's Garden' one afternoon after having squid for lunch. A telegram saying 'You're the best rock'n'roll drummer in the world. Come home.' brought him back two weeks later. He found his drum kit festooned with flowers.

September: Appear On The Frost Show

Ringo returned just in time for The Beatles' promotional film of 'Hey Jude' that was shown on *The Frost Show*. David Frost came to Twickenham Film Studios to record his introduction, giving the impression that the band plus orchestra were appearing live. In fact only McCartney's voice was live but the BBC (and the Musicians' Union) were fooled.

October: John And Yoko Arrested

On 18 October John Lennon and Yoko Ono were arrested at Ringo's London flat where they were living. They were charged with possession of cannabis and obstructing the police by Detective Sergeant Pilcher, an officer who specialized in busting pop stars but was later jailed for conspiracy to pervert the course of justice. When the case came to court in late November Lennon pleaded guilty and was fined £150. It was this conviction that was used by the US authorities in the Seventies to deny Lennon a residency permit.

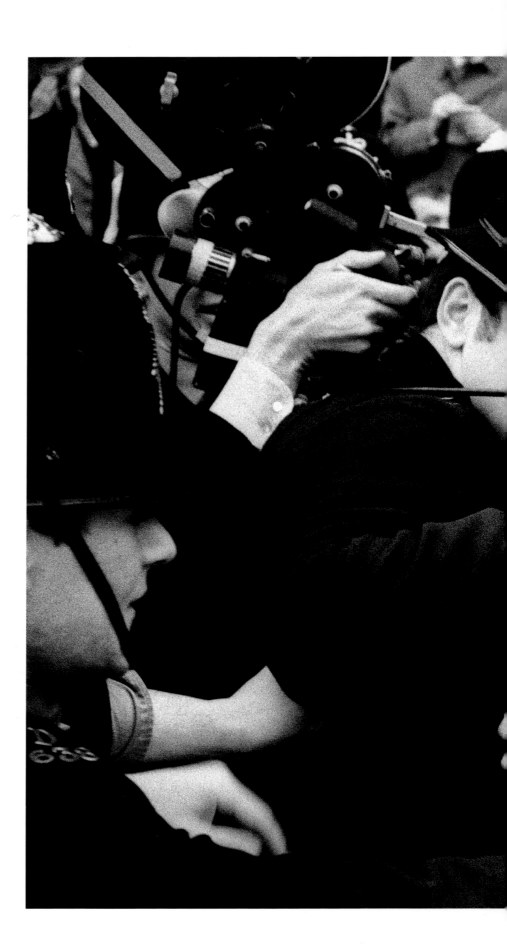

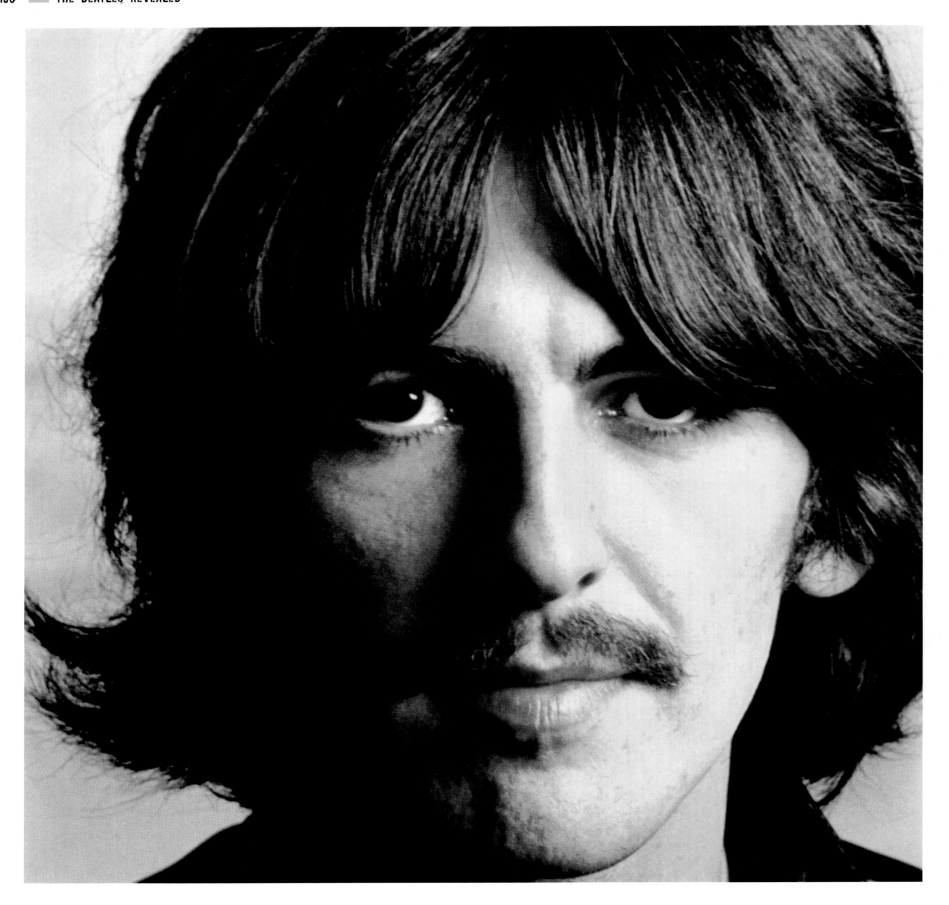

November:
George Releases Wonderwall Soundtrack

The first Apple album and the first Beatle solo album, *Wonderwall Music*, had been recorded nearly a year earlier as the soundtrack to an arty film about a voyeur called Oscar who liked to spy on Jane Birkin. George Harrison wrote and produced the score that was recorded in London and Bombay, exploring his continuing fascination with Indian music, but he didn't play or sing. The film vanished without trace.

November:
John And Yoko's Unfinished Music
No. 1: Two Virgins

Notorious for its full-frontal cover that caused the album to be sold in a plain brown wrapper – and the New York police to raid warehouses in search of it – *Two Virgins* was the experimental tape made by Lennon and Yoko on their first night together (described earlier). It featured bird calls, gastric noises (in stereo), squealing, occasional pub piano and plenty of tape effects. More people saw the cover than listened to the contents.

November: The Beatles aka The White Album

After the studio chicanery of *Sgt. Pepper* and *Magical Mystery Tour*, *The Beatles* got back to basics, focusing on songs rather than effects. More significantly, the album marked the end of the Lennon/McCartney songwriting partnership. All the songs, apart from four by George Harrison and one by Ringo, were written by Lennon or McCartney. They played on each other's songs like session musicians – and sometimes not even that. Several songs were solo efforts, although many were none the worse for it. Stylistically, *The Beatles* was incoherent compared to earlier albums like *Rubber Soul* or later ones like *Abbey Road*. But as the band neared its end it was possible to see where each Beatle could be heading afterwards.

December: The Rolling Stones Rock And Roll Circus

John Lennon played his first performance without The Beatles on *The Rolling Stones Rock And Roll Circus*, a planned TV special filmed on 11 December. He assembled a supergroup of Eric Clapton, Keith Richards on bass and Jimi Hendrix Experience drummer Mitch Mitchell. Calling themselves The Dirty Mac they ripped through 'Yer Blues' from the new Beatles album, before being joined by Yoko and violinist Ivry Gitlis for a 12-bar jam called 'Whole Lotta Yoko' featuring Yoko's soon-to-be trademark wail. Unfortunately The Stones weren't happy with their own performance and cancelled the TV special. The Dirty Mac were eventually heard when the soundtrack CD was released in 1996.

The Break-Up Years: 1969-70

1969-70

The end of The Beatles was a complex, messy affair, not surprisingly for a band that for the previous five years had been the biggest group in the world and encouraged to believe that they were divine.

The blame for their demise was cast in many directions: Yoko Ono's presence in the studio destroyed the Lennon and McCartney songwriting partnership; John Lennon showed more commitment to the peace movement than to the band; and Paul McCartney's efforts to lead the band after manager Brian Epstein's death irritated the others profoundly. George Harrison and Ringo, each of whom left the group temporarily (although news of it never got out), felt squeezed and demeaned by the other two.

But Epstein's death remained pivotal. Afterwards they showed themselves unable to manage their way out of a paper bag (although Lennon and Yoko demonstrated that they could get into one). They couldn't end it amicably and lawyers joined the other rip-off merchants who circled Apple Corps like vultures.

Occasionally the music broke through. That Lennon and McCartney could set aside their bickering and record 'The Ballad Of John And Yoko' (1969) in a day together proved the remarkable musical bond between them. The band enjoyed an Indian summer with *Abbey Road* (1969) and 'Let It Be' (1970) was a fitting epitaph, something that *Let It Be* (1970) was not.

It is no exaggeration to say that The Beatles changed the world. When John Lennon was murdered on 8 December 1980 the world stopped briefly, traumatized by the event.

1969

January: The Let It Be Sessions

After inconclusive discussions about playing a concert, The Beatles agreed instead to film rehearsals for a 'back-to-basics' album, with Michael Lindsay-Hogg who had directed their singles' promos. But the tensions that had dogged *The White Album* quickly resurfaced and the atmosphere was as cold as the sound stage at the Twickenham Film Studios. John Lennon barely spoke except to row with George Harrison who was already smarting from what he saw as Paul McCartney's patronizing attitude. The songs were in short supply and the playing was uninspired. Harrison walked out after a week and returned only after it was agreed to move the filming and recording to the band's own studio at Apple's HQ.

January: Yellow Submarine

The soundtrack album to The Beatles' full-length cartoon, released in mid-January, gathered up the four unreleased songs plus the title track and 'All You Need Is Love'. None of the other songs featured in the movie appeared. Instead, the second side of the album was filled with George Martin's film score. The album got to No. 2 in the US and No. 3 in the UK, a respectable performance all things considered. To The Beatles themselves, however, it must have seemed like a distraction from a distant eon.

January: Billy Preston

To diffuse the tensions within the band, American keyboard player Billy Preston, who had met The Beatles in 1962 playing with Little Richard and was visiting Apple to talk about a record deal, was hastily corralled into the resumed recording sessions. A lack of material had driven the band back to their beginnings to exhume songs like 'One After 909' and 'Maggie Mae'. They also tried to rekindle the flame by jamming on old rock'n'roll favourites that Preston was familiar with. They recorded onto two four-track machines borrowed from the Abbey Road Studios as the 72-track console promised by John Lennon's friend 'Magic' Alex had not materialized. He hadn't even made provision for running cables between the studio and the control room.

January: The 'Rooftop' Concert

With director Michael Lindsay-Hogg facing an inconclusive film project without a live performance from The Beatles, a hasty decision was reached. On 30 January, with the Apple staff unaware of what was happening, the band's equipment was set up on the roof of their Savile Row HQ. The Beatles played a 42-minute impromptu lunchtime concert watched by the film crew, friends, family and some lucky office workers in neighbouring buildings, but heard by many more in the streets below. Police from Savile Row Station arrived to stop the show but stonewalling tactics by the crew allowed The Beatles to finish their set, at which point John Lennon said, 'I'd like to say "Thank you" on behalf of the group and ourselves and I hope we passed the audition'. It was the last public performance they would give together.

February: Allen Klein

Having told music paper *Melody Maker* that The Beatles would be 'broke in six months' if Apple continued to lose money at the current rate, John Lennon was contacted by controversial, pugnacious New York lawyer Allen Klein who had recently untangled The Rolling Stones' financial affairs. After meeting Klein, Lennon immediately appointed him as his personal representative and persuaded George Harrison and Ringo that he should sort out The Beatles' financial mess in the wake of Brian Epstein's death. Paul McCartney preferred the father of his American girlfriend Linda Eastman, a partner in a prominent legal copyright firm, although he allowed Klein to renegotiate The Beatles' EMI contract and take a chainsaw to the overgrown Apple tree. Klein could not prevent The Beatles' priceless Northern Songs publishing company from slipping out of their control, however.

March: Paul Marries Linda Eastman

Paul McCartney first met American rock photographer Linda Eastman at London's fashionable Bag O'Nails club in May 1967. He remembered her a year later when they met at an Apple press conference in New York. She moved to London to be with him towards the end of 1968, bringing her six-year-old daughter from a previous marriage. On 12 March 1969 they were married at Marylebone Registry Office followed by luncheon at The Ritz with Princess Margaret and Lord Snowdon among the guests.

March: George and Pattie Harrison Busted

George and Pattie Harrison were late arriving at Paul McCartney's wedding reception as they had been unavoidably detained by Detective Inspector Pilcher at Esher police station where they were charged with illegal possession of cannabis. The Harrisons pleaded guilty but George claimed in court that the police evidence was a plant and that they had missed his actual stash. The magistrate accepted that the police evidence of 120 ready-rolled joints was for 'personal consumption' and fined the couple £250 each, also ordering that a pipe confiscated in the raid be returned to them.

March: John Marries Yoko Ono

Two days after the McCartney wedding John Lennon and Yoko Ono decided to get married. They inquired about a wedding at sea and found that it was not possible, so they travelled to Paris where they found that it was not possible there, either. On 20 March they flew to Gibraltar, where it was possible, flying back an hour later. On 25 March they flew to Amsterdam for a week-long 'bed-in', talking to the world's media about peace in their pyjamas. And the media relayed the message. They returned to London via Vienna where they held a press conference from inside a white bag. Finally they appeared on ITV to explain 'Bagism' on the *Today* show, but they couldn't persuade presenter Eamonn Andrews to get in the bag with them.

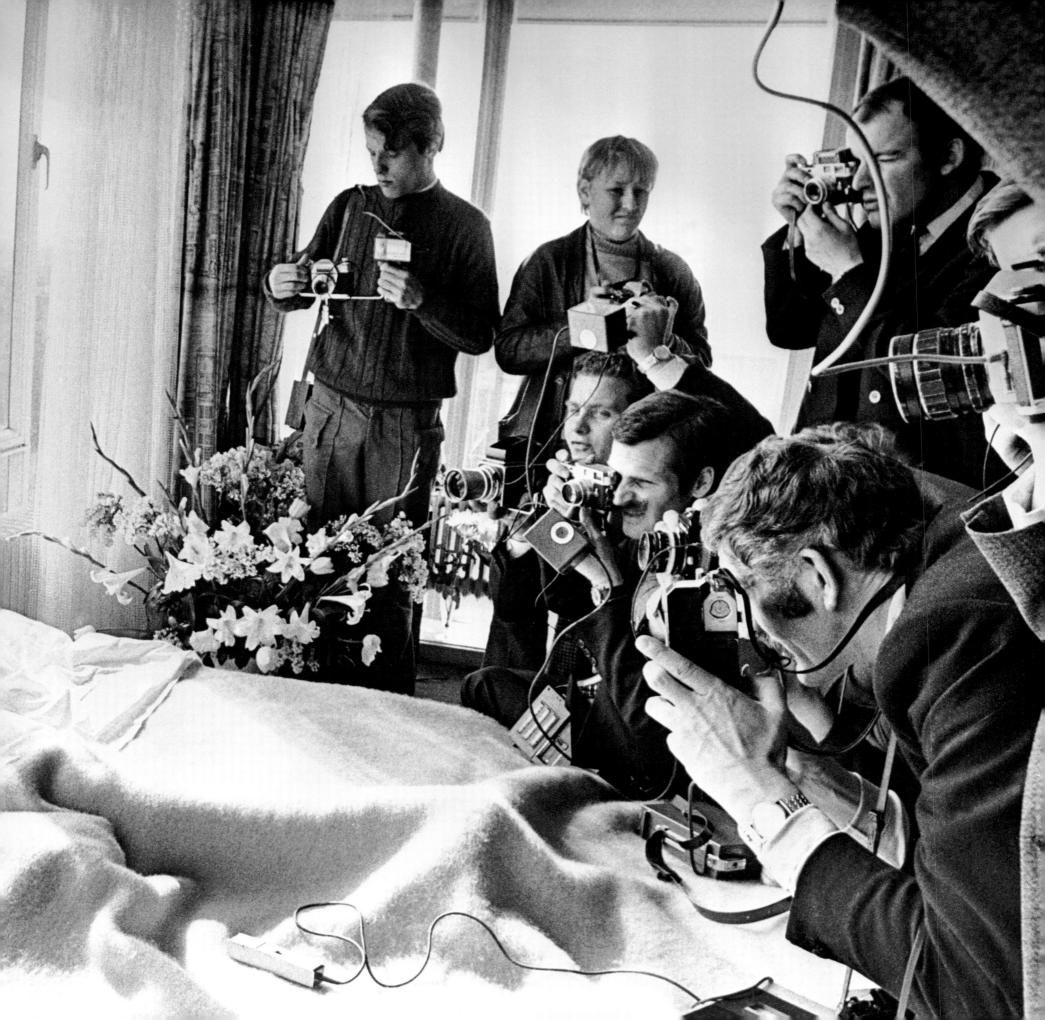

April: 'Get Back'

The first song to emerge from their *Let It Be* sessions at the start of 1969, 'Get Back' suggested that rumours of The Beatles' imminent demise were exaggerated. The McCartney rocker grew out of a jam at the Twickenham sound stage and was nailed at Apple Studios over two days. The single, another No. 1 on both sides of the Atlantic, was credited as 'The Beatles with Billy Preston', the only time the group shared their name with another artist.

May: 'The Ballad Of John And Yoko'

An unusual Beatles single, not just because it dealt with the real-life and much-publicized events surrounding John Lennon and Yoko Ono's wedding, but also because it only featured John Lennon and Paul McCartney. Once Lennon had written the lyrics and a basic chord structure he was anxious to record the song immediately. But Ringo was away filming and George Harrison was not around. So on the morning of 14 April Lennon went to McCartney's house where they arranged the song before going to nearby Abbey Road Studios where Lennon sang and played guitars while McCartney played bass, piano, drums and maracas. And George Martin produced. It was all done in nine hours. Almost like old times … almost. In America the word 'Christ' caused consternation at radio stations. Some bleeped it, others banned it, citing the line 'They're gonna crucify me' as further evidence of blasphemy. It got no higher than No. 8 in the US charts.

May: The Lennons In Montreal

John Lennon and Yoko Ono had planned another 'bed-in for peace' in New York but the US authorities denied them an entry visa because of Lennon's drug conviction. They diverted to the Bahamas, but it was too humid to stay in bed so they took off again to the Queen Elizabeth Hotel, Montreal, Canada, where they occupied three suites and continued to spread the message. On 1 June, with an array of guests that included comedian/singer Tommy Smothers, LSD guru Timothy Leary, Petula Clark, a local rabbi, members of the Canadian Radha Krishna Temple and some hastily acquired recording equipment, they recorded 'Give Peace A Chance', a populist anthem that would reverberate around the world, politically and musically.

July: The Plastic Ono Band

'Give Peace A Chance' was released by Apple Records at the beginning of July, credited to The Plastic Ono Band, the name that John Lennon and Yoko Ono had chosen for their musical

projects with whoever else was playing with them. It reached No. 2 in the UK charts but got no higher than No. 14 in the US. The Plastic Ono Band released the 'Cold Turkey' single in November 1969 followed by 'Instant Karma' in February 1970.

July–August: Abbey Road Sessions

With no one having the energy or inclination to revisit the *Let It Be* sessions and attempt to salvage an album, Paul McCartney persuaded the others that they should make one more album together and 'go out on a high note'. George Martin also agreed to produce it, provided it was done 'the way we used to'. And so they returned to Abbey Road. Sessions started in early July and McCartney had no shortage of songs and ideas, Harrison had a couple of gems on offer and Ringo had another song. But Lennon was struggling to come up with Beatles songs (as opposed to Plastic Ono Band songs) and his interest waned further when he felt that George Martin generally seemed to side with McCartney when it came to content and style.

August: The Abbey Road Cover

The photograph that would adorn the cover of *Abbey Road* was shot on the hot sunny morning of 8 August. A policeman temporarily held up traffic while photographer Ian Macmillan climbed up a step ladder in the middle of the road and took the now-iconic shot of The Beatles walking across the pedestrian crossing. The idea was McCartney's, and he chose the picture from the session.

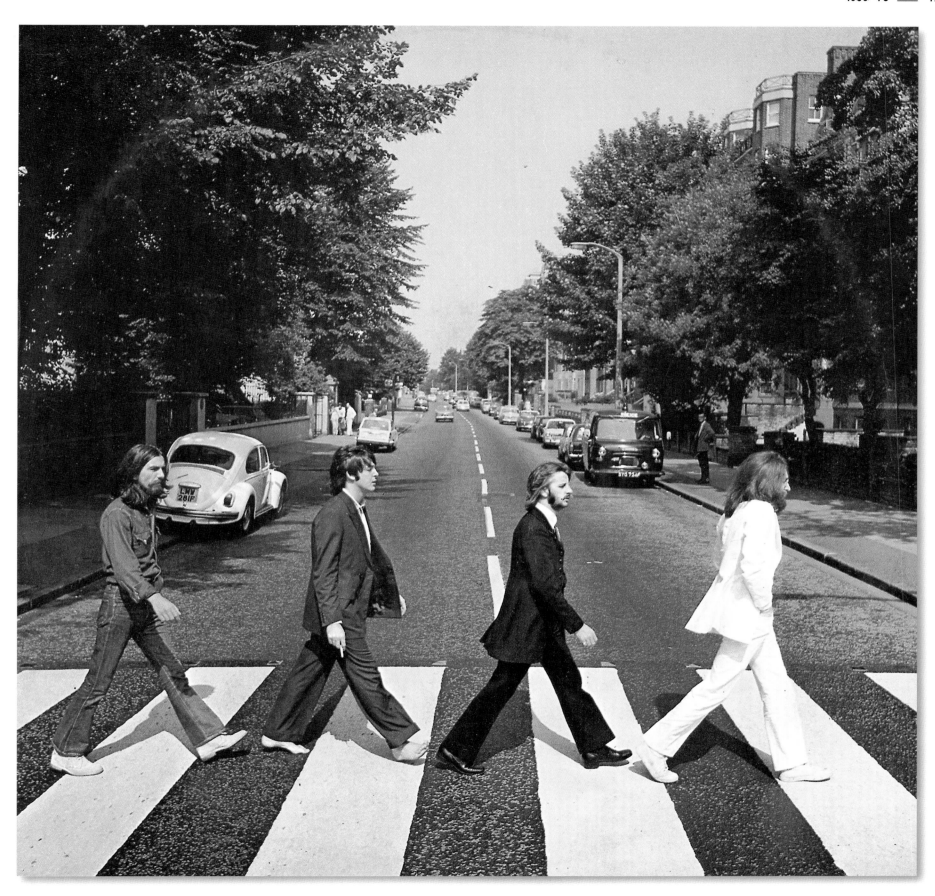

September: 'Paul Is Dead'

On 17 September the *Times-Delphic* student newspaper for Drake University, Des Moines, Iowa, ran an article by one Tim Harper suggesting that Paul McCartney was 'insane, freaked out or even dead'. There were apparently clues on the *Sgt. Pepper* cover: the mysterious hand above McCartney's head (apparently a death symbol among the ancient Greeks or American Indians, the writer wasn't sure which), the left-handed guitar in the floral arrangements, McCartney facing backwards on the back cover. Furthermore, if you played the beginning of 'Revolution' from *The White Album* backwards it sounded like 'Turn me on, dead man'. When radio stations picked up the story more clues were found, hundreds in fact. And out of them emerged the conspiracy theory: McCartney had died in a car accident in 1966 and was surreptitiously replaced by the other Beatles. Naturally, every denial from McCartney, whether flippant or serious, simply confirmed the conspiracy.

September: John's Announcement

At a meeting between The Beatles and Allen Klein to sign the new improved EMI record contract on 20 September, John Lennon, who'd just returned from playing the Live Peace Festival in Toronto with the Plastic Ono Band, told the others he was leaving. Lennon: 'It came to a point that I had to say something. So I said, "The group's over. I'm leaving". Allen [Klein] was there and he was saying, "Don't tell". He didn't want me to tell Paul even. But I couldn't help it, I couldn't stop it, it came out.' Ringo: 'If that had happened in 1965 or 1967 even, it would have been a mighty shock. Now it was just "Let's get the divorce over with" really. And John was always the most forward when it came to nailing anything.' Lennon agreed to say nothing for the time publicly for the time being.

September: Abbey Road

The last album The Beatles recorded together lived up to its pledge to 'go out on a high note', until the real final album came along. Released on 26 September, *Abbey Road* had a unified feel to it, similar to *Sgt. Pepper*, although there was no theme as such, just a slick production. The Beatles set aside their personal and business quarrels and focused on the job in hand. John Lennon's focus had already shifted elsewhere but 'Come Together' and 'I Want You (She's So Heavy)' proved he could still write great Beatles songs when he wanted. George Harrison supplied the genial 'Something' and 'Here Comes The Sun'. And McCartney's suite of songs, culminating in 'Golden Slumbers', 'Carry That Weight' and 'The End' provided a stirring climax. Meanwhile the cover was a treasure trove for the 'Paul is dead' conspiracy theorists.

October: Ringo Records Solo Album

After wondering 'What am I going to do with my life now that it's all over?', Ringo started recording his first solo album less than two weeks after *Abbey Road* was released. 'The great thing was that it got me moving … OK, let's go, not very fast but just moving in some way'. He chose a collection of standards he'd grown up listening to on the radio, and producer George Martin lined up a collection of top-notch arrangers to match. *Sentimental Journey* was released in April 1970 and reached No. 7 in the UK charts, No. 22 in the US.

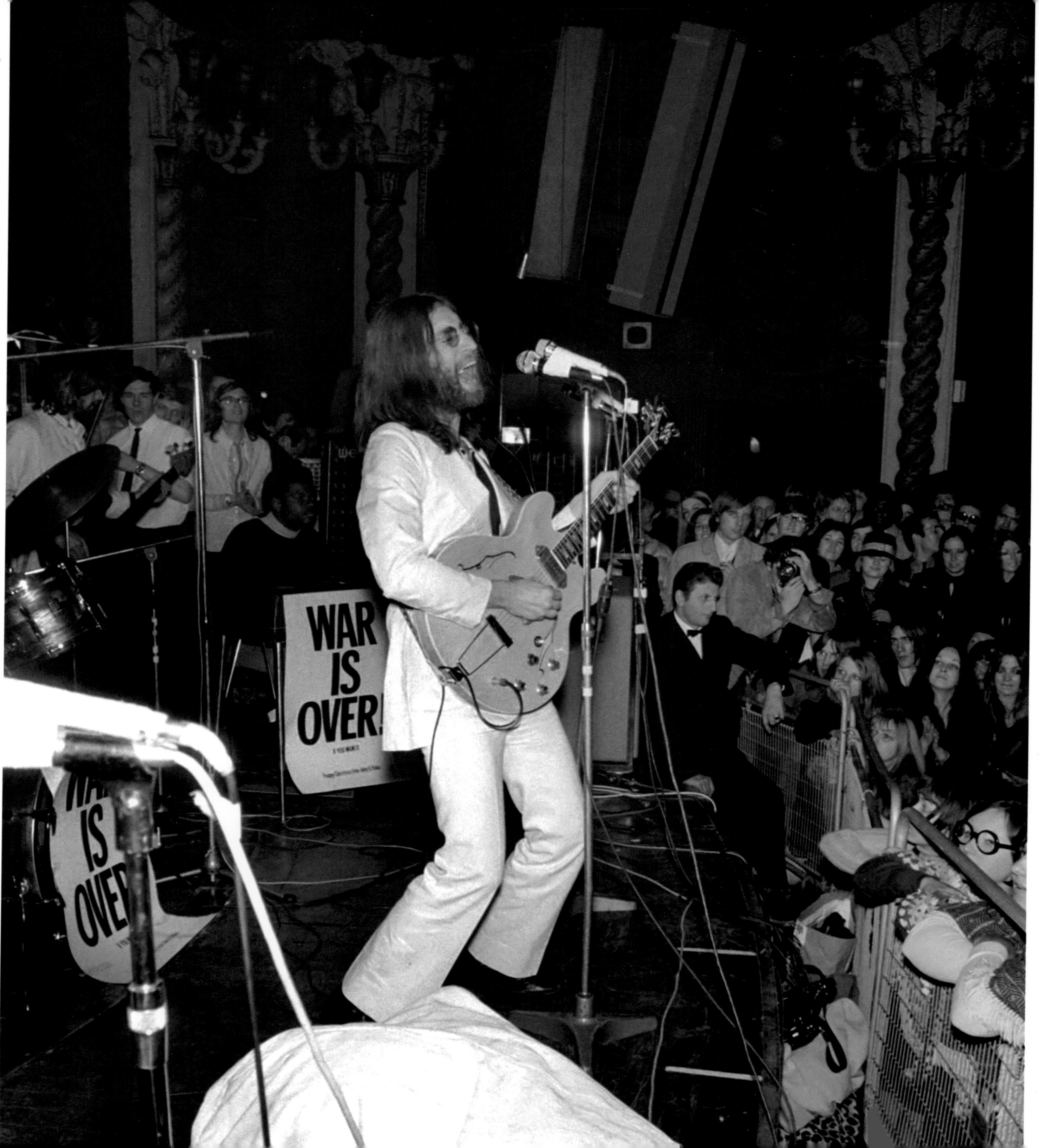
WAR
IS
OVER!

December: Lennons' Peace Campaign

As the Sixties drew to a close and the American war in Vietnam unravelled, John Lennon and Yoko unveiled an international peace campaign. They hired billboards in 11 major cities around the world and put up posters proclaiming 'War Is Over! (If You Want It) – Happy Christmas from John and Yoko'. The same message was conveyed in newspaper advertisements and leaflets. Lennon and Yoko returned to Toronto for another media blitz. Lennon: 'I'm selling a product. Henry Ford knew how to sell cars by advertising. I'm selling peace. Yoko and I are just one big peace machine.'

December: George's First Solo Appearance

With considerably less fanfare than John Lennon and Yoko, George Harrison made his first solo appearance, joining American duo Delaney & Bonnie on their British and European tour as part of their Friends backing group that also included Eric Clapton. But while Clapton was billed as a Friend, Harrison was unannounced, slipping unobtrusively on stage and relishing his role as an anonymous sideman, and when people started noticing him he ducked out of the tour.

1970

January: The Last Beatles Recording Session

On 3 January Paul McCartney, George Harrison and Ringo (John Lennon was in Denmark) gathered at Abbey Road Studios to record Harrison's 'I Me Mine', a song they had rehearsed at the *Let It Be* sessions a year previously but never recorded. Two versions of an album from the original sessions had already been rejected by the band and in March the tapes were given to legendary American producer Phil Spector. He came over to Abbey Road and spent 10 days remixing the album in his inimitable fashion. McCartney, apparently unaware of what was going on, was appalled by the lush string arrangements on 'The Long And Winding Road' but Lennon was unrepentant. 'He was given the s***tiest load of badly recorded s*** with a lousy feeling to it ever, and he made something of it'.

January: John's Lithographs Seized

An exhibition of 14 John Lennon lithographs entitled 'Bag One' opened at the London Arts Gallery on 15 January. The following day police arrived and seized eight of the lithographs, declaring them to be indecent. When the case came to court in April the magistrate ruled that they were 'unlikely to deprave or corrupt' and ordered them to be returned to Lennon. By then, of course, the exhibition was long gone.

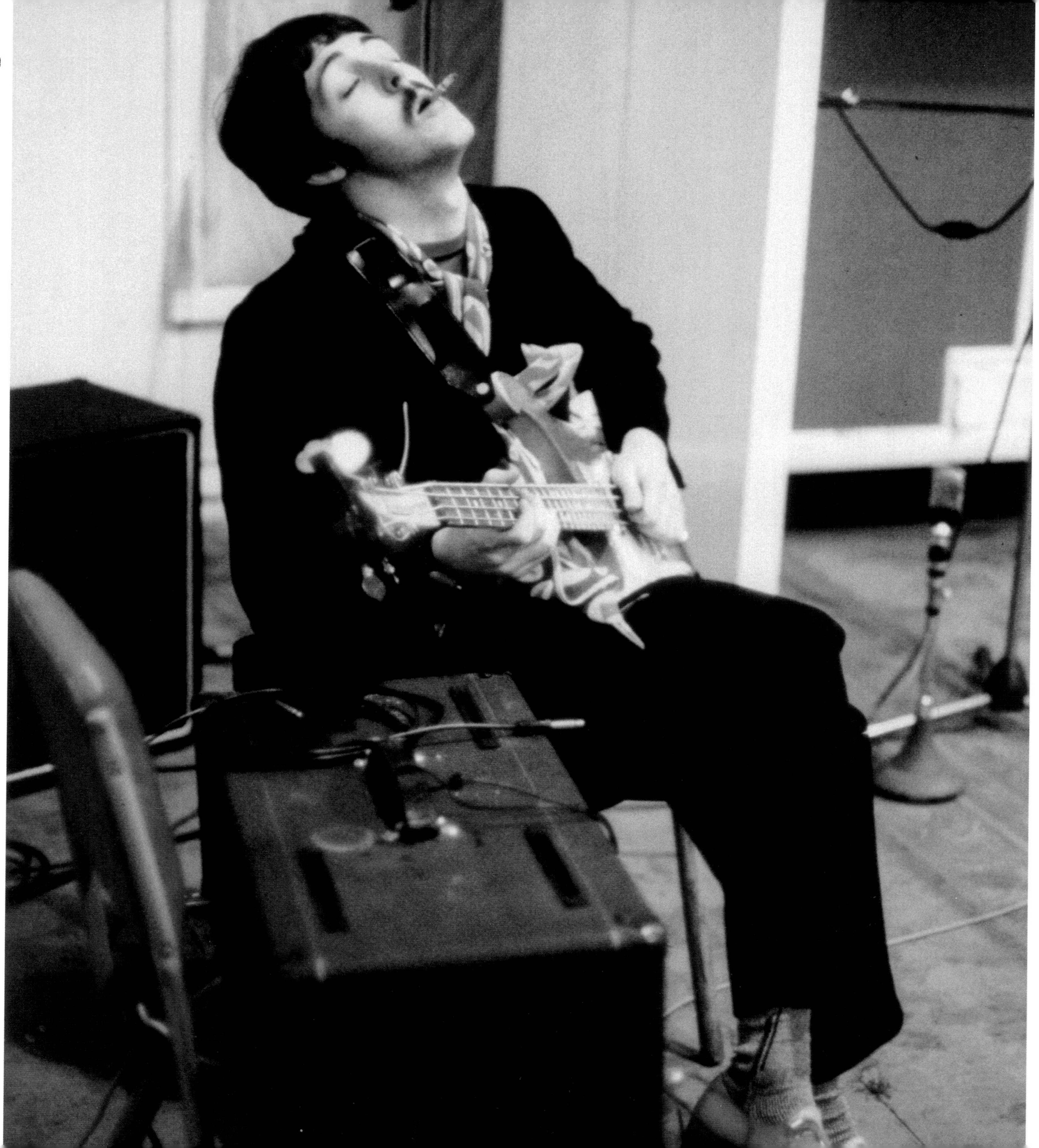

January: Paul Records Solo Album

Paul McCartney had been recording songs on his portable four-track tape recorder at home before booking time at Abbey Road Studios under the pseudonym of Billy Martin, to record his first solo album, playing all the instruments. He completed the album around the same time Phil Spector was remixing *Let It Be*. When the rest of The Beatles realized that the release of *McCartney* would conflict with *Let It Be* they asked him to move the release date. This added insult to the injury McCartney was already feeling over Phil Spector's remix.

March: 'Let It Be'

Even as The Beatles were breaking up they could still deliver a rousing anthem, or at least Paul McCartney could. His latest attempt to soothe troubled minds was given a gospel flavour, courtesy of Billy Preston's organ fills. And George Harrison took the opportunity to plug his guitar into the organ's Leslie speaker cabinet for his solo. It was a fitting requiem for the band, particularly as it did not have Phil Spector's paw marks all over it.

April: Paul Announces Split

With The Beatles now irrevocably split between Lennon, Harrison and Ringo who wanted Allen Klein to manage their affairs, and McCartney who wanted his father-in-law Lee Eastman, it was McCartney who broke ranks and publicly announced that the band had broken up. The announcement was somewhat slyly made in a press release/questionnaire to accompany his *McCartney* solo album. He blamed 'Personal differences, business differences but most of all because I have a better time with my family'. Asked whether he could foresee the Lennon/McCartney songwriting partnership becoming active again he replied 'No'.

May: Let It Be

The critical reaction to *Let It Be*, released on 8 May, was as divided as the band now were. The debate over whether Phil Spector's production saved or ruined the album has continued ever since. In 2003 Paul McCartney got his revenge when he released *Let It Be ... Naked*, removing Spector's production (and even some of his track choices) and going back to the original tapes. But some critics regarded it as a Pyrrhic victory. Regardless of the production, the real problem was that, apart from the title track and 'Get Back', the quality of the songs was well below the usual Beatles standard. And when the film came out The Beatles didn't even bother to attend the premiere.

LET IT BE

December: The Legal Conclusion

The Beatles' split turned into a divorce at the end of 1970 when McCartney sued Lennon, Harrison and Ringo to dissolve the partnership, claiming that he wanted to end the group rather than have Allen Klein diminish their legacy. The others contested the action and the case dragged on until 1975 when the partnership was finally dissolved, by which time Lennon, Harrison and Ringo were suing Allen Klein who was also suing them.

Epilogue
1970s Reunion Rumours

There were occasional rumours of a Beatles' reunion during the Seventies, usually whenever a promoter offered a preposterous sum of money for the band to reform. But there was no evidence that the offers were taken seriously. But, despite their very separate solo careers, The Beatles frequently contributed to each other's albums. Harrison played guitar on John Lennon's 1971 *Imagine* album and all four Beatles appear on Ringo's 1973

Ringo album, albeit on different tracks. In 1974 Lennon and McCartney jammed together during a session with Harry Nilsson, but the bootleg album that emerged nearly 20 years later, was aptly titled *A Toot And A Snore In '74*.

1995 Anthology

McCartney, Harrison and Ringo came together in 1995 to make the *Anthology* TV series and CD set, telling The Beatles story in their own words and compiling a six-CD set of unreleased songs, studio outtakes and rare recordings from the early days. They asked Yoko for some unfinished Lennon recordings and chose 'Free As A Bird' and 'Real Love' on which to record overdubs for two Beatle 'reunion' songs.

Index